The Kid's Guide to Exploring Nature

By the Children's Education Staff at Brooklyn Botanic Garden

Marilyn Smith, Ashley Gamell,
and Sara Epstein

with Patrica Hulse, Saara Nafici, David William Daly,
Becky Beer Laboy, and Niall Dunne

Sarah Schmidt
Editor

Laszlo Veres
Illustrator

BROOKLYN
BOTANIC
GARDEN

Parents and caregivers, please see page 118 for tips on enjoying this book with your family.

Elizabeth Peters
EXECUTIVE EDITOR

Sarah Schmidt
MANAGING EDITOR

Jason Knouft
Allison Miller
SCIENCE EDITORS

Joni Blackburn
COPY EDITOR

Elizabeth Ennis
ART DIRECTOR

Scot Medbury
PRESIDENT

Elizabeth Scholtz
DIRECTOR EMERITUS

Sonal Bhatt
VP OF EDUCATION AND INTERPRETATION

CONTRIBUTORS

David William Daly
Niall Dunne
Sara Epstein
Ashley Gamell
Patricia Hulse
Manny Jose
Barbara Kurland
Becky Beer Laboy
Saara Nafici
Marilyn Smith
Laszlo Veres

Handbook #200

Copyright © 2014, 2015 by Brooklyn Botanic Garden, Inc.

ISBN 978-1-889538-88-4 (hardcover edition)

Printed in China by Ocean Graphic International.

♻ Printed with soy-based inks on postconsumer recycled paper.

Guides for a Greener Planet are published by Brooklyn Botanic Garden, 1000 Washington Avenue, Brooklyn, NY 11225.

Learn more at bbg.org/handbooks.

The Kid's Guide to Exploring Nature

Exploring Nature

What do baby ladybugs look like? What happens to acorns when a squirrel forgets where it buried them? How do bats catch so many mosquitoes? Where do mushrooms come from?

Do you ever wonder about things like this? If so, you would make a terrific naturalist. A naturalist observes plants, animals, and other living things closely, asks questions, and tries to learn the answers. This book is full of information, adventures, and advice to help you become a naturalist.

How to Be a Naturalist

A naturalist is a scientist who studies nature. Start looking at the world through a naturalist's eyes, and you will be amazed at what you learn.

A **naturalist** studies living things by observing them and then tries to discover how they relate to each other and their environment. In earlier times, before there were many professional scientists, most of what was known about life on earth was discovered by naturalists. Today, being a naturalist takes many different forms. Field biologists, environmental educators, and scientific illustrators are all modern naturalists.

You can be one too! The chapters in this book will get you started. So will these tips.

Be quiet and still sometimes. Slow down and use your senses to listen, look, smell, and feel what's around you.

Find a sit spot. Choose a place outside that you can return to over and over again and observe. Notice how it changes throughout the day and throughout the year. Do you hear the same birds in the morning and in the afternoon? What flowers are blooming in April? In June?

Make comparisons. You are sure to see differences as you explore. How does the forest change as you hike higher up a mountain? How is one tree's bark different from another's? How do bumble bees look different from honey bees and sweat bees?

Ask questions. When you observe closely, you are sure to notice a lot of cool or unusual things: Birds with knife-shaped bills, flowers that look like bells, trees that smell like root beer. Why would that plant or animal have that trait? Does that shape, color, or smell help it in some way? Does it help it make or find food? Reproduce? Ward off predators?

Keep a journal. Buy a sturdy composition book or journal to record what you observe. On the next page—and throughout this book— you will see examples of the kinds of details you can record in your journal. Use some of the scientific words you'll see **in boldface** throughout this book. They are defined in the glossary that begins on page 114.

About the Pictures

This book's illustrations will help you learn to identify dozens of common plants and animals. They are all drawn with accurate colors, shapes, and other details. But sometimes they are made to look larger than they are in real life so that you can see these details clearly. Read the descriptions to get a sense of how big things actually are.

What to keep in your journal

Information about your surroundings:
Record the date, time, location, and weather conditions.
(Is it sunny? Has it rained lately?)

Your observations:
Choose an interesting plant. Describe it. Note its size and
color. Does it have any flowers? What do they look like?
What do they smell like? Are there any insects near the
plant? Do you hear or see any other animals nearby?
Where are they? What are they doing? Gathering food?
Hiding from predators?

Pictures:
Draw what you see, or make rubbings of leaves, bark, and
other natural objects. Take lots of photos! This is a great
way to capture and preserve an image without disturbing
the plants and animals you find.

Specimens:
Get an adult's permission to collect leaves, seedpods, and
other plant parts. (Weeds make good subjects!) Press
them between pages of newspaper under a heavy book
for several weeks, and then tape or glue them into your
journal and write about them.

Where to Explore

Look for fascinating plants and animals in the woods, at the beach, at the park, in a street tree bed, and on your window ledge.

This book is written for kids living in cities in the northeastern United States. The woods, meadows, lakes, and beaches described here are like those in natural areas of this region. You will also see some similar environments in your own neighborhood—in the park, or your yard if you have one.

If you take a day trip to go beachcombing or hiking, you may see even more of the plants and animals highlighted. Many also live in other parts of North America too. Here's where to explore.

City Nature in the city? Absolutely! You will learn a lot by observing the trees on your street, the squirrels in the park, and even the weeds in the sidewalk cracks.

Woods Forests once covered this part of the country. You can find small woodlands in large city parks, botanic gardens, and arboreta. National and state parks contain larger wooded areas. Some have been restored and include trees and other plants that once grew here naturally. Mammals like deer and chipmunks, reptiles, and hundreds of bird and insect **species** live in these woods.

Meadow Meadow plants, mainly grasses and wildflowers, grow in clearings in the forest created when trees fall or are cut. Birds, insects, and other small creatures live in them. National and state parks are likely to have true meadows. Big city parks often have meadow-like clearings that are mowed infrequently. They don't have nearly as many species of plants, but they are still good places to observe some of the same wildlife, like fireflies, bats, bees, and butterflies.

Woodland Edge The zone between woods and clearings contains plants and animals from both **habitats**. Trees and shrubs are widely spaced, and grass and wildflowers are able to grow among them. The edge of a road or trail and the shore of a lake in the forest are examples.

Lake or Pond You will see aquatic animals like ducks, fish, and turtles and plants like duckweed and water-lilies if you visit a freshwater pond or lake.

Beach There are beaches all along the east coast of the U.S., but those within state and national parks are the most likely to include a healthy shore **ecosystem** because they have been protected to minimize damage from disturbances like home building and industry.

Tools of the Naturalist

Journal

Camera

Ziploc bags

if you are in an area where it's ok to collect specimens like leaves, pinecones, and insects

Colored pencils

Magnifying glass

Writing instrument

Ruler

Chopsticks
for poking and picking up natural objects

Binoculars

Maps

Daypack

Insect repellent

available at trailheads and nature centers

Spring

Spring is a time of amazing change in nature. In March, the temperature sometimes still dips below freezing, and the trees are bare. It looks and feels a lot like winter to us, but plants and animals know that it's time to prepare for a new cycle of growth. Head outside, and you'll see flower and leaf buds swelling on bushes and trees, birds and squirrels collecting materials to build nests, and even some insects starting to move about on sunny days. By May, the season is in full swing. Notice how trees have full sets of leaves. Flowers are blooming on trees, shrubs, and other plants. Birds, insects, and other animals are busy gathering food, pairing off, and welcoming babies.

Signs of Spring

So much happens in spring. Fresh green shoots burst through dark, wet soil. Animals find mates and build nests. See if you can find these six signs of spring:

A plant that unfurls in a spiral

Green shoots poking out of the ground

Animal babies in a nest

A pollinator visiting a flower

Tiny new leaves on a bush or tree

A tree with flower buds that open before the leaf buds

Photos, clockwise from top left: Uli Lorimer, Dana Miller, Rebecca Bullene, Elizabeth Peters, Uli Lorimer, Barry Rogers

Spring Is Busting Out All Over

A sure sign of spring in the forest is the sudden appearance of wildflowers in late March and April, long before the trees grow new leaves. You might even find new flowers blooming if you retrace your path after a short walk!

Wildflowers can pop up suddenly from the forest floor because they grow from large, specialized roots that store food through winter. In spring, that stored food is used to produce leaves and flowers, which can develop much faster than they would on a plant starting from a **seed**. Spring-blooming plants need to soak up sunlight and complete their growth cycle before the trees' **dormancy** ends. Not only will trees' leaves block the sun, but their roots will also start drawing more water from the surrounding soil.

Most of these wildflowers can be seen for only a few weeks. Once the forest becomes shady, the aboveground parts wither and die, though the underground parts continue living, waiting until it's time for next year's blooms to emerge.

Insect Helpers

Most spring wildflowers develop new plants **vegetatively**, when their roots or stems grow and spread, but they also reproduce through seeds. To make seeds, they need pollen from another plant of the same **species**. This is usually delivered by insect **pollinators**. Plants have developed different flower shapes, colors, patterns, and smells to attract a variety of insects. When a bee, fly, beetle, or gnat crawls inside a blossom looking for a meal of pollen or nectar, grains of pollen stick to its body. Some rubs off on the next flower the pollinator visits, enabling that flower to perhaps make a seed.

Seed Spreaders

Many wildflowers also rely on animals to carry their seeds away so the plant can spread to new locations. Some produce edible fruits so that birds, mice, and box turtles will eat them and then "plant" the seeds after they pass through their bodies. Other spring flowers make seeds with a small, oily morsel attached. These take less energy to create than a plump berry, and ants love them. They carry the seeds back to their nest, where they eat only the oily part. They bury the seed, which eventually sprouts.

1 Bloodroot (*Sanguinaria canadensis*)
2 Canada violet (*Viola canadensis*)
3 Dutchman's breeches (*Dicentra cucullaria*)
4 Jack-in-the-pulpit (*Arisaema triphyllum*)
5 Large-flowered trillium (*Trillium grandiflorum*)
6 Mayapple (*Podophyllum peltatum*)
7 Spring beauty (*Claytonia virginica*)
8 Trout-lily (*Erythronium americanum*)
9 Virginia bluebells (*Mertensia virginica*)
10 Wild ginger (*Asarum canadense*)
11 Bumble bee (*Bombus* species)

Wonderful Wildflowers

Jack-in-the-Pulpit

Tiny flowers without petals cover this plant's central stalk and are surrounded by a leafy sheath called a **spathe**. Each one- to three-foot-tall plant is either male or female, but its gender can switch from year to year.

Arisaema triphyllum

Mayapple

The mayapple grows in large colonies of individual plants that reach about a foot tall. The young leaves look like small umbrellas as they push up from the soil, usually in early May. The plant's yellow fruit, a favorite of box turtles, ripens in summer.

Podophyllum peltatum

Dutchman's Breeches

The flowers of this ten-inch-tall plant resemble white pantaloons. They are only **pollinated** by queen bumble bees, which have tongues long enough to reach the nectar deep inside.

Dicentra cucullaria

Wild Ginger

Search below the heart-shaped leaves to find this low-growing plant's reddish-brown flowers. Wild ginger's underground stems smell like the Asian ginger plant that is used in cooking, but they are not related species.

Asarum canadense

Canada Violet

Violets are known for having purple flowers, but this **species** has white ones. It grows about ten inches high, and its **seeds** pop out of their pods and are carried away by ants.

Viola canadensis

Trout-Lily

Each flower and pair of mottled leaves of the trout-lily grows from a bulb that's at least four years old. The trout-lily grows only about four to eight inches tall and attracts ants, which carry most of its seeds away within a single day.

Erythronium americanum

Field Biologist

Field biologists are curious, adventuresome, and observant.

They must love exploring nature and reporting on what they find.

Some scientists spend most of their time in a laboratory. Not field biologists! A field biologist studies living things in their natural **habitats**. Today's field biologists usually specialize in a particular plant or animal, ferns, say, or black bears; an **ecosystem** or habitat type, like wetlands or alpine forests; or place, like the Amazon.

Field biologists collect data in different ways, depending on their specialty. Some collect samples of live plants, soil, or water. Others may record the location and number of animals in a certain area.

For example, ornithologists (bird experts) track the populations of certain **species** to ensure that they are healthy and not at risk of becoming **threatened** or **endangered**. To do this, they capture birds, place tags on their legs, release them back into the wild, and then check back after a period of time to see if their tagged birds are still thriving.

Entomologists (insect experts) often collect insects for study. They may trap them by leaving dishes of sugar water on the ground or swinging nets back and forth over bushes. Botanists (plant experts) may travel to unexplored parts of the rainforest to look for new species of plants.

Field biologists do spend some time in the lab or office compiling their findings and writing about what they've discovered. Many work for government agencies or universities. They often teach college classes and usually publish articles in scientific journals in order to share their findings with other biologists. But they always head back into the field before too long to see what else they can discover.

Ponds That Disappear

It is a dark night in March, and in a shallow pond in the forest, spotted salamanders are dancing underwater, tiny spring peeper frogs are chirping loudly in search of a mate, and hundreds of wood frog tadpoles are zooming through the water, feeding on algae.

This busy place is a vernal pond, a temporary pond that is most full in the spring. (Vernal means spring.) These ponds form in late winter when dips in the ground fill with rain and melted snow, and they dry up in the summer. Some amphibians, which spend part of their life in water and part on land, have adapted to thrive in this wet-then-dry **habitat**.

Vernal ponds are great places for many types of salamanders and frogs to breed since there are no fish, which could eat their eggs and tadpoles. These amphibians must, however, start breeding very early in the spring so that their young have time to complete their **metamorphosis** into land dwellers before the pond dries up.

Salamander Show

The best time to spot salamanders and frogs is during their spring breeding season at the vernal pond. Adults often come back to the very same pond in which they were born to produce babies. They lay eggs in the water, and the tadpoles or salamander **larvae** that hatch live and feed there.

The Transformers

As the young amphibians grow larger, their bodies prepare for life on land. Tiny legs appear on their sides, and their tails shrink until they look like miniature adults. Soon they are ready to leave the pond and move into the surrounding forest, where they'll spend most of their time under fallen leaves and logs to prevent their moist skin from drying out.

Vernal ponds don't last long. They dry up as the weather warms and the surrounding trees draw the water up through their roots. By late summer, you will see nothing but dry or damp ground where there was once a pond teeming with aquatic life. The hundreds of amphibians that once lived here will have crawled or hopped off into the forest.

1 Eastern hemlock (*Tsuga canadensis*)
2 Mountain laurel (*Kalmia latifolia*)
3 Skunk cabbage (*Symplocarpus foetidus*)
4 Raccoon (*Procyon lotor*)
5 Red-shouldered hawk (*Buteo lineatus*)
6 Spotted salamander (*Ambystoma maculatum*)
7 Spotted salamander egg masses
8 Spring peeper (*Pseudacris crucifer*)
9 Wood frog (*Lithobates sylvaticus*)
10 Wood frog egg masses

See Salamanders Dance the Night Away

Visit a vernal pond after dark, and you may see hundreds of salamanders dancing underwater. If you're lucky, you may spot some wood frogs too.

Nature centers often have naturalist-guided walks in the woods to watch as hundreds of salamanders make their way from underground burrows to the vernal ponds where they mate and lay eggs. You can organize your own expedition to a vernal pond if you know when to look and what to look for.

Spotted salamanders migrate overnight at the end of winter when conditions are wet and the temperature is above 40°F. Plan your visit within three weeks of this occurring. You will see the most activity if you visit after dark. Each person must carry a flashlight and step carefully to prevent harming the amphibians.

Search for salamanders on the ground as they walk toward the pond. Once they reach the water, male and female salamanders dance together, swimming up and down as part of their mating ritual. Shine your flashlight into the pond to see them underwater.

Each female lays a group of 50 to 125 eggs underwater. These egg masses, which are often attached to aquatic plants or debris, are one to four inches long and surrounded by an envelope of gel. They'll often be several feet from the pond edge and are easier to see during the day.

You will also probably be able to spot wood frogs at the pond. Listen for a *plop*–they tend to sit near the edge of the pond and jump into the water whenever they hear movement. They lay all of their eggs in one night. The egg masses of wood frogs aren't surrounded by an outer covering of gel like those of salamanders, and they usually float near the surface of the water like a raft.

Spring peepers may be harder to spot, but you know they are active when you hear a loud chorus of chirps at the pond.

Awesome Amphibians

Spring Peeper

This tiny frog is an inch long and has pads on its toes for climbing. When it's time to find a mate, big groups of males form a "chorus" at their breeding pond. Their high-pitched calls sound like sleigh bells and can be heard half a mile away. They chirp from late afternoon until dawn, but if you walk too close to them, they suddenly go silent, so they're hard to spot.

Pseudacris crucifer

Wood Frog

You can recognize a wood frog by the dark "mask" behind its eyes. It is two to three inches long, and its call sounds like a quacking duck. It is found as far north as the Arctic Circle, thanks to a type of antifreeze inside its cells. So it's no surprise that it can start mating even before all the ice and snow have melted.

Lithobates sylvaticus

Spotted Salamander

The spotted salamander is six to eight inches long with bright yellow spots, but this "mole" salamander is rarely seen, since it lives in burrows up to a foot deep in the ground surrounding its pond. When it's time to breed, large numbers of salamanders emerge after dark and silently walk to the pond, where they do a mating dance and lay eggs in the water.

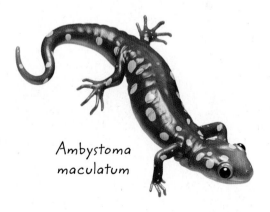

Ambystoma maculatum

Baby Animals in Disguise

Newborn animals are all around us in the spring, but most are hard to spot. That's because their parents keep them out of sight, hidden away in nests and burrows where they are warm, dry, and safe from predators.

In spring, when there's plenty of food available, many animals raise their young. But think about it: Have you ever seen a baby squirrel? These tiny creatures, called kittens, are always tucked away in tree cavities or leafy nests, where they feed on their mother's milk for months.

Baby cottontail rabbits are also hidden, either underground or in ground-level nests covered over with fur, grass, and leaves. Mother rabbits never visit during broad daylight. Why not? Because doing so might give away the nest's location to predators.

Watch for Clues

Some first-time animal parents make mistakes. They might build a nest out in the open where we can see it. This is our chance to observe the nest. Look for birds flying back and forth to one spot over and over. This could be a sign that they are building a nest or bringing food to their nestlings. You may also see birds gathering materials like twigs and leaves for their nests.

One **species**, called the tufted titmouse, even yanks fur and hair right off other creatures, like dogs, mice, and humans, so they can make a soft, warm nest for their babies. Ouch!

Other baby animals just *seem* to be disguised because they look so different from the way they will as adults. You may know that frogs start off as tadpoles, but did you know that newly hatched mosquito **larvae** look like tiny worms that wriggle around underwater? Many other flying insects, like dragonflies, also start off their lives underwater. These animal babies may not be as cute as squirrel kittens, but they are much easier to find!

Did You Know?

Many people believe that a parent bird will reject a rescued baby if it smells the human scent on it. In fact, birds have a poor sense of smell and will gladly welcome a rescued bird back into the nest.

1 Wavy hair grass (*Deschampsia flexuosa*)
2 Aphids (*Aphis* species)
3 Eastern bluebird (*Sialia sialis*)
4 Eastern bluebird nest with a cowbird egg
5 Eastern cottontail (*Sylvilagus floridanus*)
6 Eastern gray squirrel (*Sciurus carolinensis*)
7 Ladybug larva (Coccinellidae)
8 Meadow spittlebug (*Philaenus spumarius*)

Baby Animal Secrets Revealed

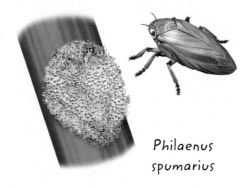

Philaenus spumarius

Meadow Spittlebug

Have you ever seen what looks like gobs of spit on plants in a meadow? This bubbly foam is actually a type of protection made by baby spittlebugs, which are smaller than grains of rice. These young insects, called **nymphs**, make the bubbles to hide themselves from enemies and to keep themselves from drying out. When the nymphs become adults, they lose their power to make spittle.

Molothrus ater

Brown-Headed Cowbird

Some birds sneak their babies into other birds' nests! The brown-headed cowbird is one example of a "parasitic nester." Instead of raising its own babies, the female lays eggs in the nests of other bird **species**. The other birds raise her chicks along with their own. It's a pretty successful strategy: Cowbird populations are on the rise.

Larva   Pupa

Egg   Adult

Coccinellidae

Ladybug

Ladybugs hatch from tiny yellow eggs and begin as **larvae** that seem nothing like the adult beetles. They look more like colorful mini-alligators! Though they may appear kind of creepy, ladybug larvae help protect plants. Just like adult ladybugs, they chow down on tiny insects called aphids, which feed on plants.

Nests Are the Best

Animals build nests for a very special reason—to start a family. Go on a walk in spring to find evidence of animals preparing to lay eggs or have babies. Notice the different types of materials used in the construction. See if you can find these animal homes:

Photos, clockwise from top left: photogrammal; Patricia Hulse, Caroline Voagen Nelson, Laurel Fan, Milan Brezovsky, Patricia Hulse

A wasp nest built with layers of papery tree pulp

A hollow tree that could be home to squirrels, birds, or raccoons

A squirrel drey built with dried leaves and twigs

A nest with baby animals in it

A bird's nest that includes both natural and man-made materials

A nest on or in the ground

Pigeons, Everywhere You Go

Even if you're not an expert bird-watcher, chances are you can identify pigeons! They're found all over our country, from coast to coast, and across the world, from the tropics to the Arctic Circle. How did these birds get to be so common in so many places?

Long ago, wild rock doves, the ancestors of the modern pigeon, lived on cliffs and in caves in Europe, northern Africa, and the Near East. As long as 10,000 years ago, people began to **domesticate** these birds and raise them for food. As people migrated to other parts of the world, they brought pigeons, too. The pigeons you see today are not truly wild but **feral**, meaning they descended from domesticated rock doves that escaped their keepers.

Happy Anywhere

Pigeons can survive in a wide range of climates, and they can eat many different foods. These traits have allowed them to live almost anywhere. Their wild ancestors nested in treeless rocky areas and fed on seeds that fell to the ground. Sometimes they scavenged in nearby fields for grain that farmers left behind. You can see how cities, with their clifflike buildings and plenty of food on the ground, suit pigeons just fine.

Pigeons mate for life, and one pair can raise up to six broods each year. They build flimsy nests hidden away on window ledges or under eaves, and the female lays one or two eggs at a time.

Both parents take turns sitting on the eggs, and once the babies hatch, both parents feed them by regurgitating a fatty fluid called crop milk into their beaks. They grow quickly, and after about a month, the young pigeons, or squabs, look just like adults and are ready to leave the nest.

Did You Know?

Pigeons have an amazing sense of direction. Even if they are taken very far from home, they can use the earth's magnetism to find their way back. In earlier times, before telephones and computers, people trained pigeons to carry messages home quickly. Soldiers used homing pigeons in this way to warn each other when enemy armies were planning attacks.

1 Adult rock pigeon (*Columba livia*) and chicks
2 Blue-bar pigeon
3 Checker pigeon
4 Pied pigeon
5 Red pigeon
6 White pigeon

Birds of Many Feathers

Have you ever noticed how many colors and patterns there are in pigeon plumage? This common bird has some striking variations.

Most pigeons are predominantly gray, but some are reddish brown, white, or black. And the gray pigeons usually also have patches of other colors, like purple and green. The way these colors are arrayed is also very diverse. These variations are called color morphs.

You can study these differences. Go to a spot where you've seen pigeons hanging out before. Bring some birdseed and scatter it around, and see who shows up. Keep a tally of all the different color morphs you see. Which ones are the most common?

Blue Bar
Dark head and tail, iridescent neck and chest, light gray body, and two dark stripes on each wing

Checker
Dark head and tail, gray speckled pattern on wings and back, wings may have bars

Pied
White patches anywhere on the body

White
No special markings

Spread
Very dark gray to black, metallic patch on neck

Red
Reddish-brown coloring over most of the body

What Are These Pigeons Doing?

Courting

A male pigeon courts a female by puffing his neck feathers up, lowering his head, and fanning his tail while he struts around in a circle. He may "drive," or run closely behind the female. If she accepts him, they will nuzzle each other's necks and "bill"—the female puts her beak inside her mate's as they bob their heads up and down.

Flocking

Pigeons are social birds, seeking safety in numbers. Whether roosting, eating, or flying, flocking together in large groups helps deter attacks by larger birds such as red-tailed hawks or peregrine falcons. In flight, pigeons take turns leading the flock, veering and swooping at speeds of up to 40 miles per hour.

Feeding

Watch a flock of pigeons feeding—it looks like a frenzy. But they're not competing. If you scatter assorted birdseed and watch closely, you'll see that each bird is concentrating on a particular kind of seed. And if one pigeon discovers a new food source, it will share that information with the rest of the flock.

For the Birds

Visit the beach in spring, and you won't see many sunbathers yet. But you will see thousands of shorebirds gathered together along the shoreline, eating, flapping, calling, and vying for a prime location to forage for food. Where did they all come from, and what are they doing here?

There are always birds at the seashore, but there are never as many—or as many different kinds—as there are during spring. You might see a dozen different kinds of bird in one glance. Many are **endangered** or **threatened species**.

Among them are **migratory** shorebirds that fly thousands of miles north to their breeding grounds every year. Some species, like the red knot, the ruddy turnstone, and the sanderling, fly all the way from Central and South America to the Arctic tundra! They must use the beaches of the mid-Atlantic as a stopover to rest and eat.

Perfect Timing

The horseshoe crab, a hard-shelled sea creature that has been around since the time of the dinosaurs, provides food for many of these migrating birds. Just as these hungry birds are arriving along the east coast of the United States, horseshoe crabs are coming ashore to lay billions of soft, protein-packed eggs. Most eggs end up being eaten, but because so many have been laid, some will survive to hatch into tiny horseshoe crabs.

Staying Put

Other migratory birds, like piping plovers and black skimmers, have reached the end of their journey once they get to the coasts of New Jersey, New York, and New England. These birds will stay here for the summer instead of going farther north because these beaches are their nesting grounds. They are now busy finding mates, building nests, and preparing to raise their young.

Resident birds like the herring gull and the American oystercatcher are also around. They live along the coast year-round. In the spring they become more active as they start looking for mates and defending their territory.

---

1 American oystercatcher (*Haematopus palliatus*)
2 Black skimmer (*Rynchops niger*)
3 Dunlin (*Calidris alpina*)
4 Herring gull (*Larus argentatus*)
5 Horseshoe crab (*Limulus polyphemus*)
6 Piping plover (*Charadrius melodus*)
7 Red knot (*Calidris canutus*)
8 Ruddy turnstone (*Arenaria interpres*)

Help Rebuild Shorebird Habitat

You can help restore sand dunes, a fragile habitat for shorebirds. While you're at the beach, you're sure to be treated to remarkable spring birdwatching.

All winter at the beach, storms bring strong winds that push waves far onshore. These waves erode the sand dunes, endangering the fragile dune **ecosystem**. Every spring, professional conservationists and volunteers restore damaged beach **habitat** by planting American beachgrass, which helps stabilize and rebuild the dunes. You can help too.

Early spring is the best time to plant American beachgrass because its roots are still dormant. Many conservation groups organize weekend events in which volunteers help plant the grass. It may take more than 5,000 plugs of grass to cover a damaged dune, but with many people helping out, it will take no time at all. Volunteers also sometimes remove **invasive** plants and pick up litter as part of the effort.

A healthy dune system is the basis of a healthy seashore. A healthy seashore offers the best chance for survival for wildlife that depends on it for food and shelter.

One conservation group that organizes beach restoration along the East Coast is the American Littoral Society (littoralsociety.org). There are also many local groups devoted to a specific park or beach. Keep an eye out for beach restoration events in March and April.

Three Fine Feathered Friends

Red Knot

This little bird migrates all the way from Chile to the Arctic Circle! It must stop to refuel along the Delaware Bayshore. The red knot relies on horseshoe crab eggs even more than other birds do. They are this bird's only food on its stopover. For years, people overfished horseshoe crabs, so there aren't many left. As a result, the number of red knots dropped so far that the bird became an **endangered species**. Strict regulations are now in place to protect both the horseshoe crab and the red knot.

Calidris canutus

Piping Plover

In the spring, the piping plover arrives on northeastern beaches and builds its nest in blowouts, U-shaped recesses in the dune made by winter winds. It lays its eggs in a scrape, a depression it makes in the sand. Camouflage is the main form of protection for the piping plover's young. Both the eggs and the chicks are sand colored. When predators approach, the chicks stay very still to go unnoticed.

Charadrius melodus

American Oystercatcher

This species must live along the coast because of its food preferences. As you might guess, the oystercatcher loves oysters, but it also eats mussels, clams, crabs, and even starfish. It can use its long bill as a shovel to dig for clams, as a knife to probe inside tightly closed shellfish, and as a hammer to crack open shells.

Haematopus palliatus

Life on the Rocks

Rocks are always under our feet. Though they're not living, they help make life on earth possible. They are the building blocks of the planet.

Rocks form the structure of mountains, valleys, and shores. Rocks were smashed and pressed into these landscapes millions of years ago. They were pushed up from underground, melted and reshaped by volcanic eruptions, and carved into by glaciers, huge sheets of ice that once covered much of the land on earth. The glaciers also pushed huge piles of rocks around the continents as they moved.

The earth's outermost layer of solid rock is called bedrock. Much of the land is bedrock covered with layers of loose stones and soil that support forests, meadows, and other **ecosystems**. But there are places where the bedrock is exposed, like cliffs and mountaintops.

Soil and Sunbathing

Rocks are made of minerals, and as they slowly crumble, the minerals become part of the soil. Plants take up minerals, and then animals like us eat those plants. You've probably heard that our bodies need minerals like iron and calcium—those come from rocks!

How else do rocks support life? Many living things live on, in, or under them. Some birds, like peregrine falcons, nest in crevices of cliffs. Insects and other tiny creatures sometimes shelter under small rocks. Cold-blooded animals like snakes and turtles often lounge on sun-warmed stones to heat up their bodies.

Plants sometimes grow on bare rock too. Many ferns and mosses thrive on shady, wet stones, and trees can send their roots right over boulders to reach the soil. The flaky brown, green, or orange crust you sometimes see on rocks is also a living thing—two living things, actually—called **lichen**. Lichens are made up of algae and fungi that partner up to live on rocks or trees. The algae gather energy through **photosynthesis**, and the fungi absorb moisture and minerals.

Did You Know?

Lichens are so sensitive to air pollution that scientists use them to judge the surrounding air quality. If you see lichens, then the air you're breathing must be pretty clean!

---

1 Rock cap fern (*Polypodium virginianum*)
2 Rosette lichen
   (*Phaeophyscia rubropulchra*)
3 Scaly dog lichen (*Peltigera praetextata*)
4 Common garter snake
   (*Thamnophis sirtalis*)
5 Five-lined skink (*Eumeces fasciatus*)
6 Gneiss boulder with ribbon of quartz
7 Manhattan schist outcropping

Rocks That Will Knock Your Socks Off

Mica

Mica is a mineral. Sometimes it is found on its own, as a glittery, flat rock that can be peeled into layers. It is also found in combination with other minerals. Mica is used in paint, walls, and even makeup. It's the secret ingredient added to New York City sidewalks to make them sparkle.

Quartz

Quartz is a shiny mineral that usually looks like milky-white or pinkish crystals. Quartz is also often found in combination with other rocks. It can look like a white ribbon wrapped around the rock or like many sparkling specks embedded in it. Most sand is made up of tiny grains of crushed quartz. Quartz sand, or silica, is used to make glass, used for everything from computer screens to windows to drinking glasses.

Schist

Sparkly schist contains both mica and quartz. It is formed by heat and pressure deep underground and then shoved up to the earth's surface. Tall buildings can only be built on very hard rock, like schist, that can hold their weight. New York City's skyscrapers are built on top of a strong, durable layer of this rock called Manhattan schist.

Nature Educator

Nature educators are great communicators who know tons about nature and ecology.

They must love plants, animals, and people of all ages.

Has someone ever shown you an amazing animal up close at the zoo? Or taught you to identify birdcalls on a nature walk in the woods? Or dissected an interesting flower so that you could see what it looks like inside? That person was probably a nature educator.

For these teachers, a zoo, beach, camp, or hiking trail can be their classroom. They usually teach kids—and sometimes adults—about the natural world by showing them actual examples of plants and animals, often in their natural **habitat**.

People can learn a lot about nature by reading books, but to really understand how a living thing looks and behaves, nothing beats a live example. Zoos, parks, and public gardens often have professional nature educators on staff to show visitors around, teach workshops, and lead demonstrations.

Some nature educators also put together the exhibits in visitor centers or along trails. Others may work at summer camps or school gardens, where they may teach classes on an ongoing basis.

Nature educators often do a lot of writing as part of their work. They may write brochures, guides, or books. In fact, the book you are reading was written by a team of nature educators!

By teaching kids about nature, these educators help inspire them to care deeply about living things and their habitats. These students can then go on to become environmental stewards, people who work to protect the planet for generations to come.

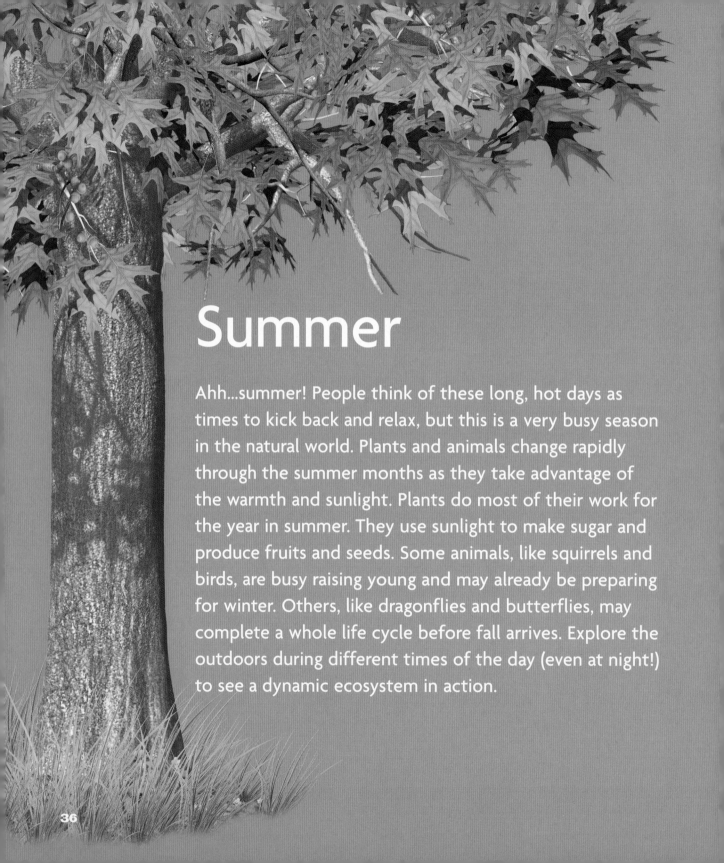

Summer

Ahh...summer! People think of these long, hot days as times to kick back and relax, but this is a very busy season in the natural world. Plants and animals change rapidly through the summer months as they take advantage of the warmth and sunlight. Plants do most of their work for the year in summer. They use sunlight to make sugar and produce fruits and seeds. Some animals, like squirrels and birds, are busy raising young and may already be preparing for winter. Others, like dragonflies and butterflies, may complete a whole life cycle before fall arrives. Explore the outdoors during different times of the day (even at night!) to see a dynamic ecosystem in action.

Signs of Summer

As the weather warms and the days grow longer, you will see many changes in nature. See if you can find these six signs of summer:

A leaf bigger than your hand

A bee visiting a disk-shaped flower

A butterfly visiting a flower cluster

A spider sitting in a web

A cricket chirping

A plant other than a tree that's taller than you

Photos, clockwise from top left: Rebecca Bullene, Elizabeth Peters, Uli Lorimer, U.S. Department of Agriculture, John Beetham, Rebecca Bullene

On Top of the Water

The surface of a pond is a special world where air and water meet. Water-lilies bloom here, dragonflies lay eggs, and ducks eat one of their favorite foods, a tiny, bright green floating plant called duckweed.

Zoom in and you'll see that what looks like a blanket of green is actually thousands of tiny duckweed plants, each with a single root dangling below. Ducks love to eat it, and so do other waterfowl, as well as muskrats, beavers, and frogs.

Water-lilies, smartweed, and spatterdock grow up through the water from roots anchored in the muck at the bottom. Their floating leaves make good resting spots for dragonflies and other small creatures. Pond snails and water mites live on their underside.

How are these plants able to spend their lives in and on top of the water? They have special **adaptations** like spongy, air-filled stems, which carry oxygen down to the roots below. They also have broad leaves to increase the surface area available for **photosynthesis**. Their **stomata**, tiny openings in the leaves where carbon dioxide and oxygen pass through, are on top of the leaves instead of on the underside, as with most plants.

A Busy Surface

Darting among these floating plants are tiny springtails and water striders, which are held up by the water's surface tension and never get wet. Fishing spiders wait on the pond's edge until they feel the ripples from a passing insect and then dart out to catch and eat it.

Meanwhile, on the underside of the pond surface, tiny pond snails glide along upside-down and mosquito **larvae** hang, each breathing through a tube on its tail that extends just above the water's surface like a snorkel.

Did You Know?

Ponds and lakes are similar but not exactly the same. A pond is often fed by a single small stream and is fairly shallow and still, making it possible for aquatic plants to cover its surface. Larger and deeper, a lake may be fed by several small streams or one big one and can have currents, so plants grow only along the shore.

---

1 Duckweed (*Lemna minor*)
2 Fragrant water-lily (*Nymphaea odorata*)
3 Smartweed (*Persicaria amphibia*)
4 Duckweed firetail (*Telebasis byersi*)

5 Fathead minnow (*Pimephales promelas*)
6 Fishing spider (*Dolomedes triton*)
7 Freshwater snail (*Sorbeoconcha physidae*)

8 Mallard duck (*Anas platyrhynchos*)
9 Mosquito larvae (*Culex* species)
10 Water strider (*Gerris remigis*)

Build a Boat That Stays Afloat

How is it that some aquatic plants and insects are able to grow or walk right on top of the surface of the water?

Insects like water striders stay afloat on top of a pond or lake because of surface tension. Surface tension exists because water molecules stick very tightly to each other when they are next to air molecules. It's almost as if the molecules form an invisible skin.

Visit a pond and conduct an experiment using natural objects like leaves, twigs, acorns, sticks, and pinecones. Which float? Which sink? Can you construct a boat that floats using only the materials you find at your feet? Which materials work best?

Amazing Aquatic Plants and Animals

Dragonflies and Damselflies

Many **species** of dragonfly and damselfly spend the majority of their yearlong life as **nymphs**, living just under the surface of the water. They are usually adults for only a few weeks. During this time, females deposit their eggs underwater, usually on a stem or under a leaf of an aquatic plant.

Telebasis byersi

Smartweed

You may have seen similar plants growing as weeds in the park or in your yard. Those are a closely related species of smartweed. Why do you think this aquatic smartweed has wider leaves than its relatives on land?

Persicaria amphibia

Fragrant Water-Lily

Try to get out early in the day to see this water-lily. It opens its flowers and smells most fragrant in the early morning and then closes up for the day around noon.

Nymphaea odorata

Water Strider

Striders hunt for aquatic invertebrates. They grab their prey with their front legs, then suck out their juices using a sharp mouthpart called a rostrum.

Gerris remigis

Spatterdock

This plant looks a lot like a water-lily, but it has bright yellow flowers. (Water-lilies are usually pink or white.) If the water level drops, spatterdock's more rigid stems hold the leaves above the water, while water-lily stems bend so that the leaves stay afloat.

Nuphar advena

Duckweed

Duckweed survives cold winters by forming special buds called turions in autumn. They sink to the bottom of the pond and lay dormant over the winter. When the water warms in the spring, they float back to the surface and develop into new plants.

Lemna minor

What's That Smell?

Many woodland plants make delightful scents to attract pollinators, like the magnolia, which has sweet-smelling flowers to draw beetles. So why do many other plants produce strange or even awful smells?

Smells can be a powerful defense. Since plants can't run away from the animals that eat them, they have other ways to defend themselves. Some have thorns. Others contain deadly poisons. But many plants are able to fend off pests just by smelling bad. Just as we use strongly scented bug spray to ward off mosquitoes, these plants have their own built-in repellents—natural chemicals that protect them from pests. Many not only smell terrible but also taste terrible to insects, rabbits, deer, and other animals that eat plants.

To the Rescue!

Some plants can even use smells to call for "bodyguard" insects. For example, when a beet armyworm caterpillar begins chewing on the leaf of a corn plant, the corn plant recognizes the caterpillar's spit. It then releases a special scent that attracts a certain **species** of wasp that attacks the beet armyworms. The wasps soon arrive to rescue the plant!

Skunks and Stink Guns

Many animals also produce nasty smells as a way of warning predators, "I taste terrible. Don't eat me!" When a tiger swallowtail caterpillar is threatened, it raises a red "stink gun" that looks like antlers and oozes foul-smelling goo. Some ground beetles spray putrid chemicals when attacked by predators like toads.

Toads use smell to defend themselves too. They give off a scent to repel snakes, owls, and skunks. And of course, when a skunk is threatened, it shoots a stinky fluid from the base of its tail. It can shoot up to 15 feet, hitting the predator with a nasty musk that stinks for days!

This strategy works against most predators, but there is always something willing to eat a stinky meal. Great horned owls dine on skunks regularly. Why doesn't the unpleasant scent bother them? Probably because these birds have almost no sense of smell.

---

1 Sassafras (*Sassafras albidum*)
2 Spicebush (*Lindera benzoin*)
3 Sweet-bay magnolia (*Magnolia virginiana*)
4 Sweetgum (*Liquidambar styraciflua*)

5 Wintergreen (*Gaultheria procumbens*)
6 Brown marmorated stink bug (*Halyomorpha halys*)
7 Great horned owl (*Bubo virginianus*)

8 Spicebush swallowtail butterfly (*Papilio troilus*)
9 Spicebush swallowtail caterpillar
10 Striped skunk (*Mephitis mephitis*)

Make Your Own Bug Spray

You can use the power of plant defenses to concoct a homemade insect repellent that really works. Mosquitoes beware!

The scents and flavors of our favorite kitchen herbs actually ward off many insects. You can use these plants to make homemade bug repellent. Many herbs and spices will work—see which ones you have at home and sniff them to decide which combination you like. Bug-repellent herbs and spices include basil, chives, cloves, coriander, cinnamon, lavender, lemongrass, lemon balm, mint, thyme, rosemary, and sage.

Ingredients and Supplies

2 sprigs (or 2 Tablespoons, if dried) each of several kinds of bug-repellent herbs or spices

1½ cups of apple cider vinegar

Empty pint jar with lid

Empty spray bottle

Instructions

1 Pour the apple cider vinegar into the jar.

2 Add the herbs and spices you choose.

3 Screw on the lid and shake the jar thoroughly. Then place it where you will see it every day. Label the empty spray bottle with the date and the ingredients and set it aside.

4 For the next two weeks, shake the jar of vinegar and herbs for a few minutes each day to release the plant oils into the vinegar.

5 After two weeks, fill the spray bottle with equal parts water and your herb solution. Shake it up to mix and apply to your skin.

Warning: This bug spray may smell very strong for the first few minutes.

Smells That Repel

Sassafras

The bark, leaves, and roots of this tree smell like root beer. In fact, root beer was originally made from its roots. Even though people like its fragrance, most insects can't stand it, which means sassafras has few pests to worry about. But there is one insect called the spicebush swallowtail caterpillar that loves spicy leaves and is happy to munch on sassafras. You can identify sassafras by its three different leaf shapes—a football, a mitten and a ghost.

Sassafras albidum

Brown Marmorated Stink Bug

Like other stink bugs, this insect oozes a smelly liquid from its body when threatened. Most predators lose their appetite when they detect the foul odor. If they do try eating the stink bug, they will find the taste horrible. This bug originally came from Asia, and here in the United States, only a few predators are willing to eat it. As a result, it has become **invasive**. It is running rampant on our farms, threatening crops like apples and peaches.

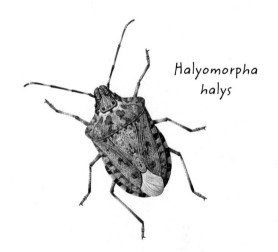

Halyomorpha halys

Sweetgum

This tree contains a powerful, bitter-tasting resin or "gum" that discourages insects and also helps the tree heal its wounds. It flows like sap inside the tree, oozing out wherever the bark is broken. You can identify a sweetgum tree by its spiky fruits and hand-shaped leaves that smell sweet and spicy when crushed.

Liquidambar styraciflua

Hoots, Chirps, and Wing Beats

Take a walk through the meadow after dark, and you'll hear and see plenty of night life. Many creatures only come out now because it's harder for predators to snatch them up.

These animals are nocturnal, which means they rest in hiding places during daylight and wait for the cover of darkness to come out and find food. Meadow voles venture out to find seeds and leaves, porcupines come out and chew tree trunks to get to sap, and beetles crawl out of hiding to munch on leaves. Some of these animals will even avoid coming out during a full moon because the brighter moonlight makes them easier to spot.

Looking for Love

A meadow on a warm night is a symphony of trilling, buzzing, tweeting, and bellowing. Why? Many male insects, birds, and amphibians call to attract mates in the dark, when it's safer to advertise their location. Some of the tiniest of these creatures play the loudest, using special body parts like musical instruments. The cricket chirps by rubbing a "scraper" located above one wing over a spiny ridge atop the opposite wing. Imagine running a pencil across a comb.

The American toad has a pouch in its throat that it can inflate like a balloon to make its trilling calls. The katydid, a relative of the cricket, rubs its front wings together to make a call that is so high pitched that it sounds like a hiss to us. Other katydids can hear it clearly with special ears located on their front legs.

Night is not entirely safe, though. Nocturnal hunters like owls, raccoons, skunks, and opossums have **adaptations** of their own that help them hunt insects, rodents, and other prey. Some have huge ears and eyes that give them powerful hearing and night vision to help them find dinner in the dark.

Did You Know?

You can tell the temperature by counting cricket calls! Some crickets get more active as the temperature rises. Count the number of chirps for 15 seconds and add 37. The total will be very close to the temperature in degrees Fahrenheit.

---

1 Evening primrose (*Oenothera biennis*)
2 Barn owl (*Tyto alba*)
3 Field cricket (*Gryllus pennsylvanicus*)
4 Little brown bat (*Myotis lucifugus*)
5 Meadow vole (*Microtus pennsylvanicus*)
6 True katydid (*Pterophylla camellifolia*)
7 White-lined sphinx moth (*Hyles lineata*)

Speak to the Fireflies

All you need is an ordinary flashlight and the secret codes below to communicate with fireflies on a summer night.

A firefly's light is caused by a chemical reaction in the rear of its body, called the "lantern." Males use a special code by altering the timing and length of flashes as they fly. Each firefly **species** has its own pattern of flashes to attract a mate of the same species. Females perch in the grass. If a female is interested, she responds, usually with a single flash.

Try impersonating a male firefly. Head to a grassy area on a warm evening with a small flashlight, and use this chart to identify some common firefly species. Use your light to flash one of these patterns a few times in a row. Watch to see if anyone flashes back at you from the grass!

	Eastern Firefly (Photinus pyralis)	Pennsylvania Firefly (Photuris pennsylvanica)	Say's Firefly (Pyractomena angulata)
Flash Pattern	½-second flash every 6 seconds	1 flash every 7 seconds, alternating between short (¼-second) and long (2½-second) flashes	Series of 8 fast flashes every 3 seconds
Flash color	yellow	green	orange
Notes	The males make a J-shape by flying upward with each flash.	Some females impersonate other firefly species to trick—and then eat—them.	Males are often the victims of the female Pennsylvania firefly.

Nocturnal Navigators

White-Lined Sphinx Moth

Like many moths, the white-lined sphinx moth is a nighttime **pollinator**. Many flowers open at night specifically to attract moths. Some of these flowers are bright white so they can be seen in the dark. Many release perfumes, another way to attract insects at night. Moths navigate by using the moon. Have you ever seen a moth circling an electric light? It has probably mistaken the light for the moon and become confused.

Hyles lineata

Barn Owl

A barn owl can circle silently above a pitch-black field at night and hear a tiny mouse below. It then dives down and expertly scoops up its prey. One secret to the barn owl's success: One ear is placed high up on its head and the other is lower. This helps it calculate prey location by sound alone. The barn owl's eyes are also twice as sensitive as ours, but it can only look straight ahead! Like all owls, it must turn its head to look around.

Tyto alba

Little Brown Bat

Bats use echolocation to find their insect prey. They send out high-pitched sounds and then listen to how they bounce off surrounding objects. This works on prey as tiny as a fruit fly. A single little brown bat can find and eat thousands of mosquitoes in one night! We usually can't hear a bat's sounds, but some insects can. Moths will zigzag to escape approaching bats, and some beetles and crickets make loud clicks to confuse them.

Myotis lucifugus

The Urban Forest

The trees that line our streets are an important part of the landscape of the city. They make our neighborhoods more pleasant and help us connect with nature. They also help the environment in ways that may surprise you.

You've probably noticed that tree-lined blocks are beautiful. Trees' shady canopies keep the city cooler in the summer, and they also provide **habitat** for urban wildlife like songbirds and squirrels. Urban trees also provide a lot of benefits that might not be so obvious. They provide oxygen and trap pollutants in the air, such as ash, dust, and smoke. That helps us all breathe a little easier!

Like all plants, trees release water through their leaves, which also cools the air. This is called transpiration. A mature oak tree can transpire 40,000 gallons of water in a year. The roots of city trees can absorb a lot of rainwater during heavy storms. This helps prevent the sewer system from flooding and carrying pollutants and sewage to our rivers and oceans.

Tough Customers

Compared with forest trees, street trees must be able to endure a lot of stress. The soil in their little sidewalk tree bed tends to be nutrient-poor and can get really compacted from people walking on it. Setting up a tree guard around the tree bed will help keep foot traffic away. Adding mulch will help return some nutrients and organic matter to the soil. Urban trees must also be able to tolerate drought, floods, and pollution like the salt that some cities use to melt snow and ice.

At Home in the City

A lot of thought goes into planting street trees. Most cities employ tree experts called arborists to select good candidates. One of their jobs is to choose the right tree for the right spot. They have a lot to consider.

How tall and wide might the tree grow over its lifetime? Will it have enough space? Will it interfere with overhead utility lines? Will it get enough sunlight? How much water does it need? Once the proper tree is selected and planted, it's up to neighborhood tree stewards like you to look after it!

1 Honey locust (*Gleditsia triacanthos*)
2 Pin oak (*Quercus palustris*)
3 Downy woodpecker (*Picoides pubescens*)
4 House sparrow (*Passer domesticus*)
5 House wren (*Troglodytes aedon*)
6 Rock pigeon (*Columba livia*)

Become a Tree Steward

Newly planted street trees need someone like you to help them settle into their new home and grow into healthy, mature trees.

During the first five to ten years after being transplanted, street trees need to be cared for by a steward, someone who looks after them. If you have a young street tree in your neighborhood, here are some ways you can help it grow.

Water This is one of the best things you can do for your tree, especially in the first two years, before its root system has spread out. Young street trees need from 15 to 20 gallons of water a week. That's about half the volume of a bathtub.

Mulch Spreading a two-inch layer of wood chips or shredded bark mulch around the tree bed will help retain water and add nutrients to the soil as it **decomposes**. Be sure not to mound the mulch up against the trunk.

Make signs A homemade sign can educate your neighbors about what you're doing and why it's important. You could also remind people not to litter or chain their bikes to the tree. Include the tree **species** on your sign and a fun fact about street trees. Maybe you'll inspire other people to be tree stewards too!

London Plane Tree
Gardeners on duty: Paloma, Max and Yasmin
Please curb your dog!

Get to Know Some Common Street Trees

Honey Locust

This tree is **native** to North America and has feathery, **compound leaves**, which means they are divided into many leaflets growing from one stem. Some leaves are even doubly compound, which means they are divided twice.

Gleditsia triacanthos

Ginkgo

The ginkgo tree has existed since the time of the dinosaurs. Some ginkgo trees are male and some are female. Male plants make pollen and female plants make **seeds**. With ginkgos, you notice the difference in autumn, when female trees drop their smelly, soft, light orange seeds.

Ginkgo biloba

London Plane

The leaves of the London plane can be mistaken for maple, so make sure to also look for the characteristic exfoliating bark, which peels off, leaving a pattern that looks like military camouflage.

Platanus x acerifolia

Pin Oak

Pin oak leaves have deep, U-shaped divisions and pointy tips. Like other oaks, the pin oak makes acorns that take two summers to mature. Can you think of a common city animal that relies on the pin oak for food?

Quercus pallustris

Norway Maple

The Norway maple has wide, five-lobed leaves. If you break the leaf stem, you'll see milky sap inside. We now know that this **species** is **invasive**. In forests, its leaves block sunlight from the saplings of native trees like the sugar maple. You will still see Norway maples in many cities because they were planted before this problem was discovered.

Acer platanoides

Callery Pear

This species of pear is planted for its beauty, not for its fruit. It has lovely white flowers in the summer, and its leaves turn shades of red and purple in the fall. Its tiny pears are hard and sour, but birds love them. They eat these little fruits and spread the tree's seeds far and wide. Because of this, the Callery pear is also becoming invasive.

Pyrus calleryana

Working Together

Plants, animals, and other living things are connected by special relationships. Many help each other out, but a few cheat!

Living things are dependent on each other in all sorts of ways. How did they come to be linked? Over many generations, organisms that live in the same **ecosystems** have slowly changed, or **evolved**, along with each other. As a result, they now have all kinds of special traits, or **adaptations**, that help them survive and reproduce. These adaptations can help or hinder other **species**' chance of survival.

Visit a flower patch in summer, and you might see monarch butterflies on the fragrant pink flowers of milkweed plants. The butterflies help the plants make **seeds** by moving pollen from one flower to another. In exchange, the plants provide monarchs with a meal. They produce the nectar that the butterflies sip from the flowers. A close relationship like this is called **symbiosis**. Some symbiotic organisms are so intimately linked that one lives inside another!

Poisonous Protection

The symbiotic relationship between monarchs and milkweed goes beyond **pollination**. Most animals stay away from milkweed because of its toxic white sap. Not monarch butterflies! They have evolved to handle the toxins, and in fact will only lay their eggs on milkweed leaves. When the caterpillars hatch, they eat the toxic leaves, making their own bodies poisonous to predators. This protects them so that eventually they **metamorphose** into butterflies that pollinate more milkweed flowers.

Milkweed provides the same protection to milkweed bugs and beetles. The flower clusters are also foraging **habitat** for some creatures. Crab spiders hide out here and capture visiting insects. Below them, long-legged harvestmen wait to catch any scraps the spiders drop.

Unfair Trades

Symbiotic relationships often benefit both partners, but not always. Some organisms have evolved ways to take advantage of others. For instance, "nectar robbers," like carpenter bees, steal nectar from flowers without pollinating them. Some flowers also trap their **pollinators**! It may not seem fair, but in nature, these organisms often get ahead.

---

1 Common milkweed (*Asclepias syriaca*)
2 Flower crab spider (*Misumena vatia*)
3 Harvestman (*Phalangium opilio*)
4 Milkweed aphids (*Aphis nerii*)
5 Milkweed bugs (*Oncopeltus fasciatus*)
6 Monarch butterfly (*Danaus plexippus*)
7 Monarch caterpillar
8 Monarch cocoon

Some Symbiotic Relationships

Quercus species
and Sciurus carolinensis

Oak Tree and Eastern Gray Squirrel

When squirrels collect acorns in the fall, they end up planting a lot of oak trees. The squirrels first eat the acorns that have been nibbled by insects, because those acorns will rot soon. Squirrels bury the intact acorns, which hold up longer as stored food. Those are also the ones that will successfully grow into oak trees, and this is exactly what happens to the acorns the squirrels forget about.

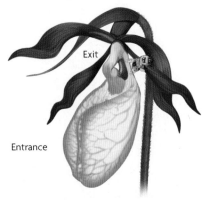

Exit

Entrance

Cypripedium acaule
and Bombus vagans

Pink Lady's Slipper and Bumble Bee

Pink lady's slipper orchids have **evolved** to cheat their **pollinating** partners! Their flowers smell like sweet nectar. Hungry bees push their way between the scented petals, only to find themselves trapped inside the pouch-shaped flower, with no nectar to be found. To escape, the bees must push their way out through a tiny hole. As they do, they get covered in pollen, which they carry to the next lady's slipper flower.

Ants and Aphids

Many ant **species** farm tiny insects called aphids, much like humans raise cows. Aphids make sweet "honeydew" with the sugar they suck from plants. Ants eat the honeydew, and some even "milk" the aphids by stroking them with their antennae. In exchange, ants protect the aphids from predators and bring them to food. Some ants even build shelters for aphids out of leaves and keep their eggs warm in their own nests.

Formica species
and Aphis species

Taxonomist

Taxonomists are observant, careful, and detail oriented.

They must love classifying plants, animals, fungi, or other life-forms.

There are more than one million known **species** of living things on earth, and each one has a carefully chosen scientific name. This name helps tell scientists how it is related to other living things and how it evolved from its ancestors. A taxonomist is an expert in classifying and naming species.

The system we use to classify plants, animals, and other organisms was developed by a naturalist named Carolus Linnaeus 250 years ago. Living things are divided into families (like the aster family), **genera** (like the coneflower genus), and species (like the purple coneflower) based on certain traits, like height, leaf shape, or flower type.

To make it easier to keep track of everything, Linnaeus developed a two-name labeling system. Each organism has a Latin species name that includes its genus (*Echinacea* for all coneflowers) and a modifier, or epithet, to distinguish it from other species in the genus (*Echinacea purpurea* for the purple coneflower).

In earlier times, scientists placed an organism in a category by carefully observing it. Today, taxonomists also study DNA, genetic material inside an organism's cells. This helps them figure out how different species evolved from their ancestors. Early naturalists were surprisingly accurate at classifying species just by using traits they could observe. Still, DNA shows that some organisms that seem closely related actually evolved from different ancestors, and taxonomists are constantly reevaluating these classifications.

Scientists think there are seven million undiscovered organisms—not counting bacteria—yet to be found deep in the oceans and in unexplored corners of the planet. This ought to keep taxonomists busy for a while!

The Buzz on Bees

Visit a patch of flowers on a sunny day, and you are bound to see and hear bees. If you pay close attention, you'll notice that there are actually many different kinds—round, fuzzy bumble bees, tiny green sweat bees, big black bees, and bees with amazing patterns.

New York City alone is home to more than 200 **species** of bee! The plants all around us rely on these bees to spread their pollen so that they can make **seeds**. We humans also rely on them because they **pollinate** many of our food crops.

The bees that make the honey we buy at the market are just one kind of bee, the European honey bee. Farmers brought them to North America in the 1600s. The **native** bees that were already here don't make honey. And most don't live in a big hive with other bees like honey bees do.

Cuckoos and Cutters

Native bees usually live alone, in small holes in wood, inside plant stems, or in the ground. They have as many different lifestyles as they have shapes and sizes. Leaf-cutter bees cut pieces of leaves and use them to build their nests. Lemon cuckoo bees steal pollen from other bees' colonies instead of collecting it from flowers. Most native bees have tiny stingers but do not use them unless their life is threatened. Why should they? They have no colony or honey stores to defend. If they do sting, it is much less painful than a honey bee or wasp sting.

Shake It!

Scientists have discovered that most bees actually pollinate flowers by buzzing. What you hear when you hear a bee buzz is the sound of it shaking its whole body.

When a bumble bee visits a tomato blossom, for instance, it grabs on and shakes like crazy until a cloud of pollen covers its body. The bee cleans up and gathers most of this pollen to carry back to feed its young, but some gets left on its body. This gets carried to the next flower the bee visits. Now the flower has been pollinated, which means it might produce a delicious tomato for us to eat!

1　Eastern prickly-pear (*Opuntia humifusa*)
2　Mountain mint
　　(*Pycnanthemum tenuifolium*)
3　Purple coneflower (*Echinacea purpurea*)
4　Blue-green sweat bee
　　(*Augochlorella* species)
5　Eastern bumble bee (*Bombus impatiens*)
6　Eastern carpenter bee (*Xylocopa virginica*)
7　Leaf-cutter bee (*Megachile* species)

Bee Behavior Stakeout

Why is one bee flying in circles and another diving face-first into a flower? Watch closely, and you may be able to decode their mysterious behavior.

On a sunny, warm day, find a spot with many flowers blooming and look for bees. Follow one bee with your eyes for as long as you can and note what it is doing. Get close enough to see its legs, eyes, and tongue. Draw and describe it. Next, make a chart. On the left side, describe the bee's behavior. On the right side, guess why the bee is doing what it's doing. Is it defending its territory? Looking for food? After you've observed a few different types of bee, ask yourself—do different bee **species** behave differently? Do bees do different things at different times of day?

August 5, 2:30 p.m.

Bee #1
Appearance: Large, fat, and fuzzy with yellow and black stripes.

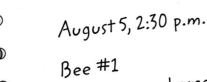

I observed:

It makes a loud sound, dives into the center of a yellow flower, face first.

It flies around in circles up above the flowers. Globs of pollen (?) are stuck to its legs.

It rubs its eyes and

I think...

It might be buzz pollinating.

It's looking for a place to land or watching for enemies.

It may be cleaning itself or scratching itself.

Bees to See... and One Wasp!

Eastern Bumble Bee

This is one of the easiest **native** bees to spot. It is large, round, and fuzzy, and it **pollinates** many of our important food and flower plants.

Bombus impatiens

European Honey Bee

You have probably seen a lot of these bees, which have a fuzzy thorax and a yellow and black striped abdomen. This is the **species** of bee that produces honey and beeswax. If you see one, there may be a beekeeper's hive nearby.

Apis mellifera

Eastern Carpenter Bee

This bee looks a lot like a bumble bee, except that its abdomen is smooth instead of fuzzy. It bores holes in wood to make its home. A carpenter bee may be big and loud, but it doesn't sting.

Xylocopa virginica

Leaf-Cutter Bee

The dark body and yellow belly of the leaf-cutter bee makes it easy to identify. Leaf-cutter bees collect pollen on their bellies instead of in pouches on their hind legs like other bees.

Megachile species

Blue-Green Sweat Bee

This bee is tiny and shiny and looks more like a fly than a bee. Farmers love sweat bees because they pollinate food plants like strawberries, tomatoes, and watermelons.

Augochlorella species

Eastern Yellow Jacket

The yellow jacket is actually not a bee at all—it's a wasp. Like bees, yellow jackets drink nectar, but they also eat insects. You can tell a wasp from a bee by looking closely at its body. Wasps have very skinny waists and smooth bodies.

Vespula maculifrons

Wonder Weeds

Walk down a city street, and you will see plants growing everywhere: in sidewalk cracks, in tree beds, along the edges of buildings, in empty lots. They're weeds, of course—the toughest, wiliest plants in the world.

Most people think of weeds as a nuisance, but they are also pretty amazing plants. They have the power to live almost anywhere and can survive in tiny patches of dirt where they are trampled by people, blasted with car exhaust, and peed on by dogs!

These wild plants weren't planted by a gardener. Instead, they planted themselves. Is that what makes them weeds? Not necessarily. A weed is simply a plant you don't want growing in a certain place. A rosebush growing in the middle of a lawn could be considered a weed if you wanted only grass there.

Super Spreaders

Weeds usually show up where people don't want them because they can reproduce incredibly well. How do they do this? Some make thousands of **seeds** from a single plant. Others can regrow from a tiny bit of root left in the soil. Many spread through underground stems, called **rhizomes**. Some weeds produce fruit

for birds to eat. Inside the fruit are seeds that pass unharmed all the way through the birds' digestive system so they are able to sprout up wherever the bird leaves droppings.

Weeds sometimes produce prickly or sticky seeds that "hitchhike" on people or other animals to be planted far from the parent plant. Some weeds make feathery seeds that are carried away by the wind or on water. Some weeds do several or even all of these things.

When Weeds Invade

Some weeds are so good at spreading that they take over a large area and crowd out other plants. These weeds are called **invasive** and are considered the worst of the weeds.

Weeds tend to be the plants that people interact with the most. We're constantly pulling them out or cutting them down, but many of them were originally introduced to the area by people as food or ornamental plants!

1 Broadleaf plantain (*Plantago major*)
2 Dandelion (*Taraxacum officinale*)
3 Hedge bindweed (*Calystegia sepium*)
4 Pokeweed (*Phytolacca americana*)
5 Quickweed (*Galinsoga quadriradiata*)
6 Giant leopard moth (*Hypercompe scribonia*)
7 Gray catbird (*Dumetella carolinensis*)

Weeds You'll See Everywhere...and Why

Phytolacca americana

Pokeweed

This tall plant with dark pink stems is somewhat poisonous to people, but its berries are a healthy food for catbirds, robins, and other songbirds, which carry the **seeds** far from the parent plant. It can grow ten feet tall and has a deep **taproot** that makes it hard to completely pull out. If even a small piece of the root is left behind, it will regrow.

Taraxacum officinale

Dandelion

You will see dandelions almost everywhere. That's because they are hard to uproot and their seeds spread amazingly well. The yellow flowers turn into puffy, white seed heads containing hundreds of seeds, each one attached to a tiny, feathery "parachute" that floats away in the wind. If you've ever blown on a dandelion head, you've probably helped plant dozens of new dandelions. Dandelions also have deep taproots that can resprout even if the leaves and stems are pulled.

Arctium minus

Lesser Burdock

This plant has purple flower heads surrounded by prickly hooks called **bracts**, which act like Velcro. In fact, the inventor of Velcro probably got the idea from burdock bracts. If you brush past a burdock plant, a flower head might get stuck to you and hitch a ride away from its parent plant. It also sticks to other animals that pass by. This is how burdock is able to spread far and wide.

Weeds to See

The plants that most of us consider weeds are everywhere in the summer—in parks, sidewalk cracks, yards, and tree beds. See if you can track down these six wily weeds:

 Dandelion
(*Taraxacum officinale*)

 Quickweed
(*Galinsoga* species)

 Broadleaf plantain
(*Plantago major*)

 Sourgrass
(*Oxalis* species)

 Smartweed
(*Polygonum* species)

 Lambsquarters
(*Chenopodium album*)

Photos, clockwise from top left: Bob Jenkins, Saara Nafici (2), Wendell Smith, Saara Nafici, Ole Husby

Tough Plants for a Tough Place

Many people think the beach is one of the most pleasant places to be on a warm day. But the things we love about the beach—the sand, the saltwater, the waves, the breeze, and the hot sun—are the same things that make it a very difficult place for plants to live.

Sand is made up mostly of crushed quartz, and it doesn't have the nutrients that plants usually get from soil. The wind blows sand on top of the plants and buries them. Waves pound the shoreline, bringing tides of salty water. Salt spray also blows in from the ocean, coating plants' leaves with salt. There isn't much shade, either, so the sun beats directly down on the beach all day, heating up the sand and everything that lives there.

Fat or Hairy Leaves

Some plants do manage to grow at the beach because they have **adaptations**, special traits that help them survive and reproduce. Like many desert plants, some beach plants have extra-fat leaves and stems that can store a lot of water. They are called **succulents**. Other beach plants have leathery leaves that protect them from salt spray, which can damage the delicate tissues of plants. Some plants have leaf colors that reflect the sun's rays, such as silver or bluish gray. Others have tiny hairs on their leaves and stems to protect them from blowing sand. Look closely, and you may see several of these adaptations on many beach plants.

A Web of Life

Beach plants are an important part of the shore **ecosystem**. They create a **habitat** that provides food and shelter for birds and other animals that live here or pass through. The eastern willet is a common beach bird that builds its nest deep in the beachgrass on coastal sand dunes. This helps protect its eggs and chicks from predators like foxes, falcons, crows, and **feral** cats. Other birds, like piping plovers, nest in sandy areas that are sheltered by the grass. Butterflies and bees feed here, too, and in turn, they support the plants by **pollinating** them. Sparrows and other songbirds eat seeds and help the plants spread to new locations.

1 American beachgrass (*Ammophila breviligulata*)	3 Sea rocket (*Cakile edentula*)	5 Monarch butterfly (*Danaus plexippus*)
2 Beach pea (*Lathyrus maritimus*)	4 Seaside goldenrod (*Solidago sempervirens*)	6 Piping plover (*Charadrius melodus*)
		7 Red fox (*Vulpes vulpes*)

Where Do Beach Plants Grow?

A healthy shore ecosystem contains a variety of plants, but they don't all grow in the same place. Do some fieldwork to learn what grows where.

On a visit to the beach, draw a circle in the sand about the size of a hula-hoop near the ocean and look for plants inside. List what you see and draw pictures in your journal. Then draw another circle a little farther inland, and make another list with drawings. Then make one more observation of a nearby sand dune. Walking on the dune can harm its plants, so just draw an imaginary circle this time. Sketch and describe the plants you see growing inside. How many plants did you find in each location? Was there a difference in the type of plants, size of plants, or texture of plants growing in the different places? Why do you think these differences exist?

Date: August 25
Place: Island Beach State Park
Weather: Hot and Sunny

Circle #1: No plants

Circle #2: A short plant with light green, squishy, waxy leaves, and round seed capsules. Some purple flowers. A few blades of grass.

Circle #3: Lots of tall green grass, some tall-stemmed leafy plants with small yellow flowers.

A Few Amazing Beach Plants

American Beachgrass

The long underground stems of this plant, called **rhizomes**, spread, intertwine, and form a net beneath the sand. This holds the sand in place and helps dunes to form. As more sand blows on top of the grass, its leaves continue to grow upward, and more rhizomes spread below the new layer of sand, building the sand dune even higher.

Ammophila breviligulata

Beach Pea

This plant grows behind the dune, protected from the constant salt spray blowing in from the ocean. Its fleshy, leathery leaves withstand blowing sand and the intense heat of the sun. Its curling tendrils wind together, creating a clumping mass for protection against the harsh elements. Bees and butterflies sip nectar from its purple flowers, and birds and small mammals eat its pealike seeds.

Lathyrus maritimus

Sea Rocket

This plant avoids the blowing sand by growing and spreading low to the ground. Its **succulent** leaves and stems store water, and their waxy coating repels the salt spray. Its capsule-shaped seedpods ripen and break off from the parent plant. They land in the water and float away, carrying the single seed down the beach. All parts of this plant are edible and provide both food and stored water to shore wildlife.

Cakile edentula

Grass Like You've Never Seen

When you think of grass, you may picture a mowed, carpetlike lawn, but visit a meadow, and you'll see how varied grass is in its natural habitat. Wild grasses have narrow leaves, tiny flowers, and seed heads that look like everything from lace to caterpillars. Some grass species grow as high as seven feet!

Grasses have hollow, jointed stems and long, narrow leaves. The lower part of each leaf forms a sheath around the stem. Grasses produce flowers, though you'll have to look closely to spot them. They are usually small and surrounded by special protective leaves called **bracts** rather than colorful petals that would attract **pollinators**.

The flowers produce a lot of pollen, which is carried by the wind and lands on other grass flowers, plus everything else in its path. Once **seeds** form, they remain on the grass stalks well into autumn and winter and provide food for small birds and mammals.

A Place for Wildlife

A meadow **ecosystem** contains many different grass species as well as other flowering plants. Notice how close together the plants in a meadow **habitat** are. It can be hard for people to walk through unless someone has made a pathway, but the closely packed plants provide excellent cover for wildlife like spiders, insects, snakes, and small birds and mammals.

Grasses have **adapted** to survive fires and grazing by hungry wildlife. How do they do this? Many grow horizontal stems called **rhizomes** below the soil. If the aboveground part of the plant is eaten or burned, grass can quickly resprout from the rhizomes. Rhizomes also crowd out the roots of other plants. This helps cut down on the competition for space.

Grass also grows a bit differently than other plants. Most plants grow from the tips of their shoots or branches, but grass forms new cells lower on its stems. So even if a deer, cow, or lawnmower removes its top, it can keep growing.

Did You Know?

You probably ate some grass seed today! The grass family, called the Poaceae, is one of the most important plant families to humans because it includes grains like wheat, rice, and corn.

1 Common milkweed (*Asclepias syriaca*)	4 Timothy grass (*Phleum pratense*)	7 Indigo bunting (*Passerina cyanea*)
2 Indian grass (*Sorghastrum nutans*)	5 Eastern garter snake (*Thamnophis sirtalis*)	8 Meadow spittlebug (*Philaenus spumarius*)
3 Switchgrass (*Panicum virgatum*)	6 Eastern mole (*Scalopus aquaticus*)	9 Orb weaver spider (*Argiope aurantia*)

Go on a Grassland Safari

Grasshoppers, praying mantises, and orb weaver spiders are just a few of the wild creatures you might see in the meadow if you know how to look.

Grass flowers don't attract butterflies, bees, or other **pollinators**, but plenty of insects feast on grass stems and leaves. Grasshoppers, leafhoppers, skipper (moth) caterpillars, and spittlebugs are just a few of the insects that live on meadow plants. Praying mantises, orb weaver spiders, bluebirds, and other meadow animals hunt them for food.

Choose one grass plant in a meadow and inspect it closely for insects. Use a magnifying glass if you have one. Examine the stem and leaves from top to bottom. Don't forget to check the axils, where these parts meet. If you don't find any insects right away, check more specimens until you do.

Sketch each insect you find. Record its size and color. What part of the plant did you find it on? Can you guess how or what it might eat?

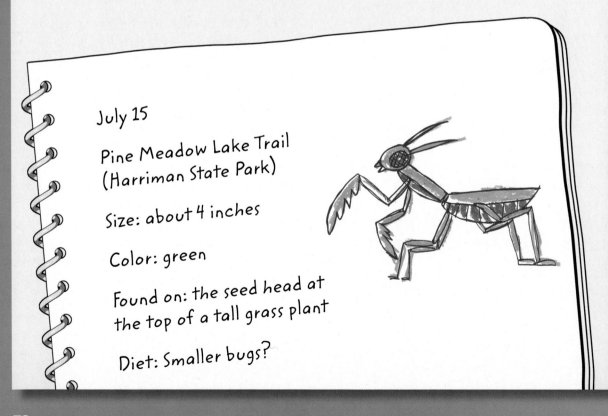

July 15

Pine Meadow Lake Trail
(Harriman State Park)

Size: about 4 inches

Color: green

Found on: the seed head at the top of a tall grass plant

Diet: Smaller bugs?

Gorgeous Grasses

Switchgrass

You can recognize switchgrass by its open, lacy flower clusters called panicles and small reddish **seeds**. It is commonly grown in cow pastures or to make hay. The stems can grow six feet high, and the dense roots grow at least that deep underground. These roots help form new sod and hold soil in place.

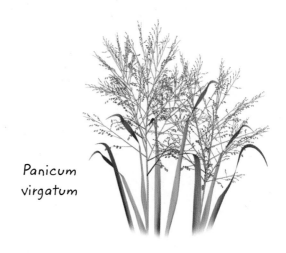

Panicum virgatum

Indian Grass

This pretty **native** species can grow up to seven feet tall. The flowers form in long, thin panicles in late summer or early fall. Each flower or seed has a half-inch-long twisted part called an **awn** and is surrounded by golden-brown silky hairs, creating a soft, furry appearance.

Sorghastrum nutans

Timothy Grass

One of the easiest grasses to recognize, Timothy grass has flowers that grow in short dense ears that look a little bit like caterpillars. The green **bract** below each flower has two tiny awns, giving the ears a rough texture. This species was brought to the United States from Europe around 1700. Rabbits, deer, cows, and horses all love to eat it.

Phleum pratense

Autumn

You will see big changes take place within a short time in the fall. Days get shorter and cooler. Animals feast on a final harvest of fruits, seeds, and nuts to prepare for dormancy or migration. Many plants are also getting ready to go dormant. The leaves of deciduous trees rapidly change color and drop, a dramatic signal that winter is on its way. Get outside throughout the fall to watch the transformation. The lush green landscape of late September gives way to bright orange, red, and yellow swaths of leaves in early November. By mid-December, not much remains but bare branches and brown stems.

Signs of Autumn

Go outside as the days get shorter and the air crisper to find evidence that plants and animals are preparing for the winter ahead. See if you can spot these signs of fall:

A shadow longer than your own

Seeds left behind on a flower stalk

Birds flying south for the winter

A leaf with many colors

Fruit that animals like to eat

A seed that travels by floating

Why Do Leaves Change Color?

The transformation of fall foliage is a spectacular event. The green leaves of deciduous trees turn brilliant colors before falling to the ground. How do trees change so dramatically in just a few weeks? And why?

Deciduous trees and shrubs are those that shed their leaves each fall and survive winter in a dormant state. That's important because their broad, thin leaves would be harmed if frozen. They would also hold heavy snow during a storm, which could cause branches to break. Dropping leaves also makes it easier to survive winter drought. A large tree's leaves lose over 100 gallons of water on a sunny day. Its roots can't replace that when the ground is frozen.

True Colors

But why do leaves change color so dramatically before falling? Color change is caused when chlorophyll production stops. Leaves are loaded with pigments that capture energy from sunlight for **photosynthesis**, the process of making sugar to feed the plant.

Green chlorophyll is the most abundant pigment in leaves, but it's not the only one. Most leaves also contain small amounts of other pigments, such as orange carotenes and yellow xanthophylls. Chlorophyll breaks down easily, but it's constantly being replaced during the growing season. When the days get shorter and the temperature drops, deciduous leaves stop producing chlorophyll. Without it, the orange and yellow pigments that have been there all along really stand out.

Some plants also start making red pigments called anthocyanins in the fall. They form on sunny days when sugar builds up in leaves. This happens after a special layer of cells starts to form a seal at the base of each leaf. When the seal is complete, the leaf detaches and drops.

Nature Recycles

After leaves fall, they continue to help sustain the forest. How? When they **decompose**, they enrich the soil. Their nutrients might even be absorbed back into the same tree from which they fell. In the meantime, they form a blanket on the forest floor that insulates the ground for plant roots and the wildlife living underground.

---

1 Black gum (*Nyssa sylvatica*)
2 Northern red oak (*Quercus rubra*)
3 Sugar maple (*Acer saccharum*)
4 Tulip tree (*Liriodendron tulipifera*)
5 Virginia creeper (*Parthenocissus quinquefolia*)

Track Leaf Color Changes

Observe one tree carefully each autumn—you may be able to see how environmental factors influence leaf color.

There are so many things that affect the production and timing of leaf colors that each fall foliage display is a bit different. If you observe one specific tree year after year and keep detailed notes, you may be able to figure out what triggers these changes.

Start by recording the date you notice the first signs of color in a few leaves. Record the type of tree, which colors you see, what percentage of the leaves have turned color, and what percentage have fallen off the tree. Check back every day or week and report the same information until all the leaves fall.

Along with your tree notes, record weather information such as the day's highest and lowest temperatures, and whether there was sun, rain, wind, or snow since your last report. Do you see any connection between the weather and leaf conditions?

You can preserve actual leaves by pressing them between pages of newspaper with a heavy book on top. Carefully arrange the leaves so they're flat, and don't let them touch each other. Use lots of empty pages in between to absorb the water from the leaf tissue. After a few weeks, the dried leaves can be glued right onto a page in your journal.

Sugar Maple in Front of My Apartment

October 15: 10% red, 0% fallen

Weather: sunny all week. Today's temp. 44° to 55°

October 21: 25% red, a few have fallen.

Weather: 2 days of rain in the past week

Lovely Leaves

Sugar Maple

This **native** tree is probably the reason that New England has a reputation for glorious fall foliage. Its three- to six-inch leaves turn bright red, orange, yellow, or all three at once.

Acer saccharum

Northern Red Oak

Oaks are among the last trees to change color each fall. The foliage of this species can turn scarlet, eventually fading to a russet brown. The brown leaves may cling to the tree all winter.

Quercus rubra

American Beech

The leaves of this large forest tree turn golden yellow, then pale brown. Young American beech trees don't shed their dead leaves until the end of winter.

Fagus grandifolia

Black Gum

This wetland tree is somewhat uncommon, so you might not see it very often. But once you do get a glimpse of its brilliant red leaves at the peak of fall, you will always remember it.

Nyssa sylvatica

Tulip Tree

This tree's five- to seven-inch leaves turn a clear bright yellow in autumn. They are easily blown off the tree by wind or rain and are among the first leaves to drop each year.

Liriodendron tulipifera

Virginia Creeper

Color change isn't limited to trees and shrubs. This common vine has compound leaves with five leaflets, which turn scarlet in early fall. You'll find it growing up tree trunks. Beware of confusing it with poison ivy, which looks similar but has "leaves of three."

Parthenocissus quinquefolia

Fascinating Ferns

It's easy to walk through the woods without noticing the ferns. They have no eye-catching flowers or fruits like other plants. But that's exactly what makes these green, leafy plants on the forest floor so special.

The first ferns appeared on earth much earlier than most plants. They are older than the trees and grasses that surround us now. Ferns were widespread during the time that dinosaurs walked the earth, and they were an important food for them. Many ferns grew as big as trees then. Some still do!

Magic "Seeds"

For many years, no one understood how ferns reproduced. During Shakespeare's time, people thought ferns made "fern seeds" that had magical powers. They thought that carrying them could make you invisible!

We now know that ferns don't make **seeds** or flowers in order to reproduce. Instead, they make **spores**. Each spore is the size of a speck of dust. Spores need lots of moisture to sprout and grow. That's why we usually find ferns in shady, damp places. After spores sprout, they live as tiny heart-shaped plantlets on the forest floor. Each one has both male and female cells.

In a film of water, male cells can swim to female cells, and an adult fern can develop.

Spores appear in late summer and autumn on the leaves of ferns, which are called fronds. Look on the underside of a frond, and you may see **sori**, the structures that hold spores. Sori look like black or rust-colored dots arranged in an even pattern.

Sometimes spores grow only on special fronds called fertile fronds. These fronds may be fuzzy or bumpy and can be green, yellow, or brown. You will often see them sticking up out of the center of the plant. On fertile fronds, spores are grouped in clusters called sporangia.

Did You Know?

Many fern plants have a structure like a slingshot around their spores. When the tiny band snaps, it shoots the spores far away from the parent plant. This gives the new ferns that eventually form more room to grow and helps these fern **species** spread to new places.

1 Christmas fern
(*Polystichum acrostichoides*)

2 Hay-scented fern
(*Dennstaedtia punctilobula*)

3 Sensitive fern (*Onoclea sensibilis*)

4 British soldier lichen (*Cladonia cristatella*)

5 Eastern newt (*Notophthalmus viridescens*)

6 North American millipede
(*Narceus americanus*)

Invisible Spores Revealed!

A single spore is almost impossible to see without a microscope. But make a spore print, and in just a few days, voilà! The spores reveal themselves.

By pressing fern fronds between sheets of paper, you can see **spores** displayed in beautiful patterns. Each type of fern will make a unique arrangement. Here's how to make one:

1 Collect a few fern fronds in late summer or early fall. Before collecting, examine the underside of each frond to make sure it has spores. They might be on some fronds and not on others. They may even be on special brown fertile fronds in the center of the plant, or hiding out on the tips or near the base of green fronds. If the fern is ready to release its spores, the sporangia or **sori** will look rusty brown.

2 Place each frond on a piece of white paper, spore-side down. Place a second piece of paper over the top of each frond. You can arrange a few fronds on a large sheet of paper to make an artistic array. Set the fronds in a dry place, where fans or breezes will not disturb them, for a few days.

3 The change in conditions from outdoors to indoors will trigger the spores to release. After a few days, carefully remove the top paper and the frond to reveal the beautiful spore design underneath.

4 You can even try planting the spores you collected. Sprinkle them onto moist soil in a small container and cover it with clear glass or plastic to keep in humidity. Place the container on a shady windowsill. Be patient, these little wonders are very slow growing!

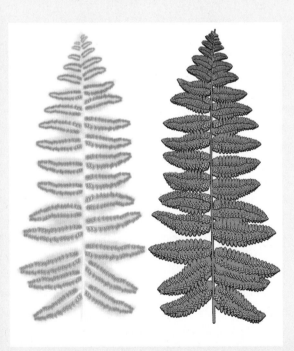

A Few Ferns to Learn

Hay-Scented Fern

The lacy, delicate fronds of this fern are light green in spring and summer and turn golden in the fall. You can use your senses of touch and smell to identify this fern. If you touch it, it will feel slightly sticky. Crush a small piece of frond in your fingers—it should smell sweet and summery, like hay.

Sori

Dennstaedtia punctilobula

Sensitive Fern

You will see sensitive fern growing along streams and ponds. Its fronds are bright lime green with chubby, round lobes. Look for its brown fertile fronds, which look like stalks covered with beads, sticking up in the center of the plant. They hold the spores.

Fertile fronds

Onoclea sensibilis

Christmas Fern

The dark green fronds of the Christmas fern feel waxy and leathery. This helps protects the plant over the winter. Its name comes from the fact that it's still green in late December after most other ferns have disappeared. Some people also think its little leaflets look like tiny stockings with the "toes" near the stem.

Polystichum acrostichoides

Why Do Trees Make Fruit?

When you think about fruits that grow on trees, you might picture delicious orchard fruits like apples and cherries. But take a closer look at the trees that line our city streets, and you'll see fruits of all kinds.

Plants make **seeds** to reproduce, of course, but why do so many of them make the fruit that surrounds them? It's the fruit's job to protect and help spread the seeds to new locations, away from the parent plant. When trees grow in a forest, their seeds stand a good chance of growing into mature trees. This usually doesn't happen on our city streets, but that doesn't stop the tree from producing fruit. Did you know that acorns, chestnuts, and seedpods are all fruits? Their structure gives you clues about how their seeds travel.

Sweet Treats

The Callery pear is a tree you'll see on many city streets. The pears it makes aren't as big and juicy as the pears we eat, but birds like them. When they eat them, they spread Callery pear seeds. Birds can only digest the fleshy fruit—the seeds pass through their stomachs and come out the other end unharmed. The honey locust, another common street tree, makes seedpods with a sweet fleshy pulp inside. Starlings eat the pulp

and scatter the hard, brown seeds. You will also find plenty of nuts like acorns and chestnuts in autumn. When squirrels collect acorns, they bury some to store for the winter. The ones they forget about may germinate and grow into trees.

Some trees, like maple, elm, and ash, make papery, winged fruits called samaras. You might know them as "helicopters" or "whirlygigs." How do you think their seeds travel? Pick one up and toss it in the air, and you'll see how!

Did You Know?

You can help honey locust seeds sprout by re-creating what would happen to them in the wild. In autumn, collect fallen honey locust seedpods. Remove the seeds and rough them up by scratching them on the sidewalk. This is called scarification and mimics what would happen if they were eaten by an animal and passed through its digestive system. Plant a few in a small pot of soil, water regularly, and see what happens.

1 Green ash (*Fraxinus pennsylvanica*)
2 Honey locust (*Gleditsia triacanthos*)
3 Pin oak (*Quercus palustris*)
4 Eastern gray squirrel (*Sciurus carolinensis*)
5 Female northern cardinal (*Cardinalis cardinalis*)
6 Male northern cardinal
7 Starling (*Sturnus vulgaris*)

Sidewalk Seeds to See

Aesculus hippocastanum

Horse Chestnut

This tree makes large green, spiny fruits. In autumn they fall and crack open. Inside each is a big, shiny brown **seed**. Sometimes there are two or three. The horse chestnut is not related to the edible chestnuts that some people like to roast. In fact they are poisonous to most large mammals, including people and horses. Small rodents can eat them, though, and they are safe to collect.

Liquidambar styraciflua

Sweetgum

Sweetgum fruits are prickly round "gum balls." In the fall they dry, turn brown, and open to release dozens of small, winged seeds to the wind. Squirrels, chipmunks, and birds eat some of the seeds, but others may find a spot to sprout.

Ginkgo biloba

Ginkgo

In the fall, when many sidewalks are littered with their squishy, smelly seeds, you will realize why this tree is nicknamed "stinko." Ginkgos are **gymnosperms**, which means "naked seeds." What you are seeing—and smelling—are not actually fruits but large, flesh-covered seeds. Ginkgos are **dioecious**, which means that each tree is either a male or a female. Only the female trees make seeds.

Horticulturist

Horticulturists are nurturing, patient, and highly knowledgeable about plants. **They must love** planning ahead, being outdoors, and getting their hands dirty.

A great garden is more than just a collection of pretty flowers or tasty vegetables. To help a garden thrive, a gardener must create a small **ecosystem** of plants.

Horticulturists are professional gardeners. They often work for cities, parks, or botanic gardens. Most of these places have gardens with themes—plants **native** to a certain area, say, or food plants, or fragrant plants. In the wild, plants grow where they do because conditions like soil, moisture levels, and surrounding plants and wildlife favor them. A horticulturist must sometimes work in reverse to create conditions that suit the plants he or she has chosen to grow.

Before planting anything, horticulturists must consider what the plants will be like when they are mature. They often raise them from seeds or very young plants, allowing them to fill the space over time. Using **ecological** knowledge, horticulturists can garden without using a lot of chemicals to fertilize plants or kill pests. Many use no chemicals at all. This is called organic gardening.

They may add compost (**decomposed** plant matter) to improve the soil. This mimics the way fallen leaves and other plant parts break down into soil in nature. Horticulturists may add plants to attract **pollinators** or bring in beneficial insects to make the garden more like a natural **habitat**. Certain wasps, for example, kill other insects that might become **invasive**.

Horticulturists also water and weed to maintain the garden as it grows and collect data on how the plants are doing in preparation for next year. It's all part of keeping their tiny ecosystem in balance as an example for everyone to enjoy.

Fun with Fungi

Deep in the forest, the kingdom of fungi thrives. Neither plant nor animal, these organisms come in all shapes and colors, with names to match their strange looks: turkey tail, dead man's fingers, earthstars, and more.

Fall and spring are good seasons to search for a variety of fungi because they thrive in cool, damp conditions. Mushrooms sometimes seem to pop up overnight, but when you see one, you are seeing just a part of the whole fungus. The rest is underground.

After a rainfall, the underground part expands incredibly fast by absorbing moisture from the surrounding soil. The fungus then sends up the mushroom to make **spores** for reproduction.

But not all fungi make mushrooms on the ground. Some species make spores in a "shelf" growing on the side of a tree or log. Some shelves are hard and woody and last for years.

Blown Away

When conditions are dry, fungi release their microscopic spores to float away on the wind. A single spore will produce a new fungus if conditions are just right where it lands. But there's no guarantee this will happen. That's why one mushroom might produce up to a billion spores!

The Fungus Kingdom

Many people think fungi are plants, but they aren't. They grow in a somewhat plantlike way—long, threadlike **mycelia** grow from their bodies. But they are actually more closely related to animals. Unlike plants, fungi can't make their own food through **photosynthesis**, so they "eat" other organisms. Instead of swallowing food as an animal does, a fungus grows on it, dissolving it with enzymes and absorbing the nutrients.

Most fungi are **decomposers**, which means they break down dead plants and animals. You will often see them on logs, branches, and other debris on the forest floor. But some fungi grow on live plants. Often fungi form a **symbiotic** relationship with plant roots, called **mycorrhizae**. The fungi help the roots absorb water and minerals, and in exchange, the roots provide nutrients for the fungi.

1 Bird's nest (*Cyathus stercoreus*)
2 Chicken of the woods
   (*Laetiporus sulphureus*)
3 Dead man's fingers (*Xylaria polymorpha*)
4 Earthstar (*Geastrum saccatum*)
5 Golden spindle (*Clavulinopsis fusiformus*)
6 Porcini (*Boletus edulis*)
7 Puffball (*Lycoperdon pyriforme*)
8 Turkey tail (*Trametes versicolor*)

Fabulous Fall Fungi

Amanita bisporigera

Destroying Angel

This plain white mushroom is common in forests and lawns. It starts as a white "button" and has deep folds called gills below its cap. The **genus** *Amanita* is famous for its many poisonous species. Some have yellow, orange, or green caps. They're a good reason to avoid eating any wild mushroom, since one bite can be fatal!

Laetiporus sulphureus

Chicken of the Woods

This striking fungus grows on trees, mostly oaks, rotting the wood to make a hollow trunk. Each "shelf" can grow up to two feet wide. They're often clustered together in a group and are very bright orange to yellow.

Lycoperdon pyriforme

Puffball

Each of these pear-shaped fungi is only one to two inches wide. Puffballs grow in clusters on dead branches or fallen trees. When young, they're white and solid inside. Mature puffballs are brown and wrinkly, with a pore, a tiny hole, in the top of each one. Why are they called puffballs? Touch one, and you'll release a cloud of olive-colored spores!

Marvelous Mushrooms

When damp weather sets in, mushrooms seem to appear overnight on trees, in mulch piles, or right in the middle of a grassy lawn. Head out after it rains to explore the diverse array of mushroom sizes, shapes, and colors. See if you can find each of these:

A brightly colored mushroom

A mushroom smaller than your pinky

A fungus growing like a ruffle on a ballerina's dress

A mushroom shaped like an umbrella

A "village" of mushroom caps

A fungus growing like a shelf on a tree trunk

Photos, clockwise from top left: Brad Henslee, Uli Lorimer, Jason Cortlund, Brad Henslee, Uli Lorimer (2)

What Happened Here?

You're walking in the forest when suddenly you notice something unusual—perhaps a clearing filled with fallen trees or an old stone wall. What happened here? Just as detectives use clues to solve mysteries, naturalists can use clues to figure out what has shaped the environment.

Have you ever come across a mossy old stone wall, winding snakelike through the woods? Much of what is now forest in the Northeast was farmland in the 1700s and 1800s. These walls are made of stones that were dug up from land cleared for the fields. Look closely. If the wall has only large stones, the field was once a pasture for grazing. But if the wall also contains smaller stones, the field was likely used to grow crops. Each time the farmer plowed, he turned up small rocks and added them to the walls.

Wild Winds Blew

You can also figure out how natural phenomena have shaped the landscape. It's common to see a fallen tree here and there, but a swath of downed trees is usually the sign of a sudden disturbance like a storm. After a major windstorm (except a tornado), fallen trees all point the same way, so you can actually tell in which direction the storm blew.

Trees with Triangles

Fires leave clues, too, like charred bark. You may also see tree trunks with triangular scars near the ground on the uphill side. That's because leaves, twigs, and other brush tend to collect on the uphill side of a tree. When they catch fire, it creates a heat vortex that burns a triangle into the bark. Some trees can't withstand fire at all and are left as blackened snags—still standing, but dead.

Changing Landscapes

In time, after any disturbance, ecological **succession** takes place. Clearings allow more sunlight to reach the soil, so **seeds** that have lain **dormant** there can grow. Fallen trees **decompose** and add nutrients to the soil, which will support the new plants—first small ones like wildflowers and grasses, then shrubs and trees. Eventually, the land will become forest again.

---

1 Eastern hemlock (*Tsuga canadensis*) snag   2 Downed red maple (*Acer rubrum*)   3 Fire-scarred red oak (*Quercus rubra*)

Become a Forest Sleuth

Do some detective work, and you may be able to figure out what happened in the woods years or even decades ago.

Lots of changes occur in the forest when few people are around to witness. Trees fall. Animals come out of hiding to eat. Fires and storms change the landscape. Some of these things happened long, long ago.

Take a hike through the woods and use your naturalist knowledge and detective skills to try to reconstruct the events of the past. When you find a clue, make a note of it. Try to guess what happened.

Clue #1: Four fallen trees lying side by side
What happened?
A big windstorm knocked them down. Probably happened a long time ago since there is a lot of moss growing on them.

Clue #2: A stone wall with big and small stones
What happened?
This area used to be a farm.

Clue #3: A light-colored tree stump with bite marks
What happened?
A beaver gnawed it down some time this year.

Clue #4: A young tree with a strip of bark missing
What happened?
A starving deer ate here during the winter.

Clues in the Forest

Stump with Bite Marks

Near a pond or lake, you might see evidence that beavers have been busy. They gnaw through tree trunks with their strong, sharp front teeth and use the logs and branches to build dams and lodges in nearby ponds. When were those beavers at work? Recently gnawed stumps are light golden. Those gnawed down more than a year ago have turned gray.

Tree with Stripped Bark

Deer don't have sharp incisors, so they won't leave bite marks on trees. Instead, they strip and eat the bark of young trees during the winter, as a last resort when leaves and tastier tender shoots are not available. This kind of tree damage might be a sign that the deer population has grown too large for the surrounding **habitat**.

Wolf Tree

A wide tree with low branches in the forest is a sign that the area was once an open pasture or meadow. Most forest trees are tall and skinny. They branch out high up in the canopy, where they are able to collect more sunlight. In comparison, a wolf tree is shorter and wider, because it grew for decades without competition from other trees for sunlight and space.

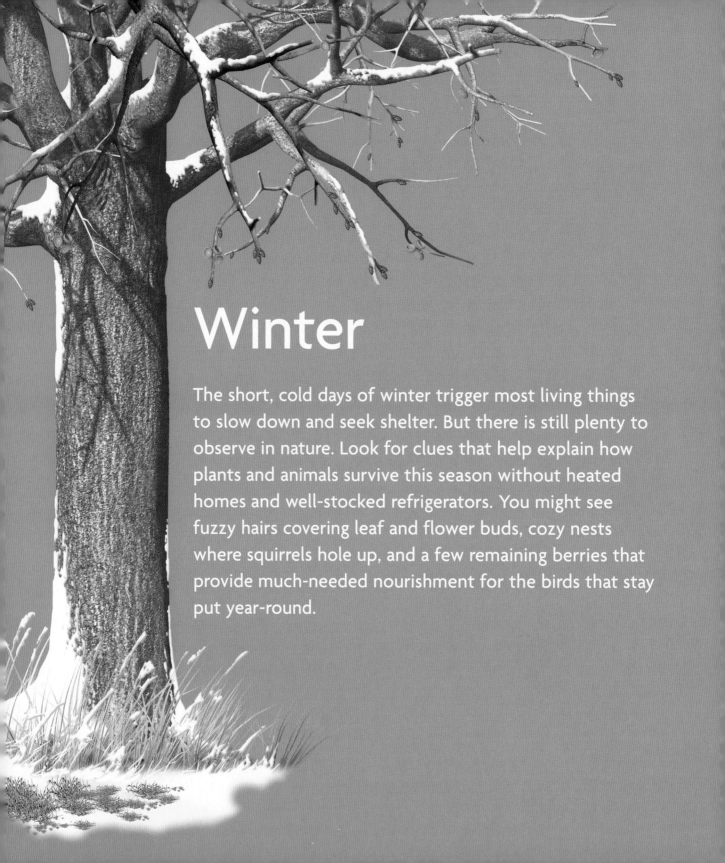

Winter

The short, cold days of winter trigger most living things to slow down and seek shelter. But there is still plenty to observe in nature. Look for clues that help explain how plants and animals survive this season without heated homes and well-stocked refrigerators. You might see fuzzy hairs covering leaf and flower buds, cozy nests where squirrels hole up, and a few remaining berries that provide much-needed nourishment for the birds that stay put year-round.

Signs of Winter

Short, cold days and long, colder nights encourage some plants and animals to go dormant through the winter. But many are alive and thriving. Look for signs of these hardy winter survivors:

Buds with leaves or flowers tucked inside

Signs of an animal meal

A winter-blooming flower

An animal that doesn't hibernate

A tree with green waxy leaves

Tracks in the fresh snow

Photos, clockwise from top left: Medi Blum, Ashley Gamell, Mike Ratliff, Doc Searls, Elizabeth Peters, Ashley Gamell

Life Under Ice

If you visit a frozen pond or lake in winter, taking a swim will probably be the last thing on your mind! But for many aquatic plants and animals, the safest place to spend winter is in the water.

The layer of ice on a lake's surface actually keeps the water below from freezing by insulating it against the frigid air. That means the water in the lake stays warmer than the surrounding land during a cold spell.

Remaining underwater is a good way for many plants and animals to survive, since only the smallest ponds freeze solid. Some algae and aquatic plants are even able to keep growing in the winter. Other plants survive beneath the muddy lake bottom or as **seeds** underwater.

Finding Food

Ponds and lakes support many mammals and birds through winter. Since they are warm-blooded, they can stay active all winter as long as they have food. Ducks, for example, often feed on plants, fish, and insects through patches of open water in a partially frozen lake or pond. If frigid temperatures cause the surface to freeze over, the ducks can't reach their food, and they must migrate south to find a warmer lake.

Slowing Down

Cold-blooded animals—amphibians, reptiles, and fish—face plenty of challenges too. Some animals that normally breathe air at the surface have to survive several months under ice without taking a breath. Turtles do this by **hibernating** in the mud at the bottom of the pond in an extremely slowed-down state. They use very little energy, so they are able to survive on the small amount of oxygen they can take in from the surrounding mud. Frogs hibernate at the bottom of the pond too, but they sometimes emerge from the mud to absorb oxygen from the water through their skin.

Fish have gills for breathing underwater, but oxygen may still be scarce. When a deep snow covers the ice on a lake's surface, it blocks sunlight. Without it, aquatic plants don't release much oxygen into the water via photosynthesis. Several species of fish have adapted to survive with very little oxygen.

---

1 Broadleaf cattail (*Typha latifolia*)
2 American beaver (*Castor canadensis*)
3 American beaver lodge
4 Barred owl (*Strix varia*)
5 Bluegill (*Lepomis macrochirus*)
6 Bullfrog (*Rana catesbeiana*)
7 Painted turtle (*Chrysemys picta*)
8 Red fox (*Vulpes vulpes*) tracks
9 White-tailed deer (*Odocoileus virginianus*)

Winter Animal Tracking

Not all animals at a lake in winter are under the ice. To look for signs left by wildlife in the snow and ice, walk carefully around the water's edge.

Here are a few tracks you might find around a lake. The size of the prints and the distance between them are important for identification. Some animals leave tail or wing tracks too.

| Rabbit | Deer | Raccoon | Muskrat | Fox | Bird |

Tracks in the snow aren't the only winter clues animals leave behind. Some of the evidence of their activity isn't easy to recognize at first, but if you explore nature in winter, you can learn to identify what creatures may have been around. *Remember: Never step on the ice!*

Owl Pellet

Nuts Gnawed by Squirrels

Muskrat Ice Trails

Animal droppings, including scat and pellets, may contain seeds, bones, fur, or fish scales. Look for them on the ground: They're important clues to the diet of the animal that passed by.

Look for signs of animal meals such as wood chips made by a woodpecker searching for insects in a tree, deer-chewed twigs, or a partially eaten nut on the ground.

If you're lucky, you might see a trail frozen into the ice itself. These are made when a muskrat, otter, or other animal moves through the ice while it is slushy. When the temperature drops, the trail is frozen in place.

Winter Wildlife

American Beaver

Though it may weigh up to 65 pounds, this shy mammal is rarely seen. But you can tell it's around when you see beaver lodges on a lake or stream and pointed stumps along the shore. These stumps are left behind when a beaver chews down trees for food and shelter. The beaver eats the tender buds and inner bark of trees. Its lodge, made from branches, twigs, and mud, has a dry room above water, but the inhabitants must still swim in and out through a doorway under the ice. Good thing they have thick fur for insulation!

Castor canadensis

Bluegill

A small sunfish, the bluegill weighs less than one pound. It prefers small lakes with lots of aquatic vegetation. In winter, bluegills keep warm by moving to deeper water, but you might see them feeding on plankton just below the ice on warmer, sunny days.

Lepomis macrochirus

Bufflehead

This tiny duck considers the northern United States a warm place to spend the winter! It flies south from Canada to spend winters here. The bufflehead duck is very buoyant, which makes it fun to watch as it dives for insect **larvae** underwater. It seems to disappear suddenly from sight, and then pops back up like a cork 10 to 20 seconds later.

Bucephala albeola

Pretty on the Outside

Do all trees look alike with their branches bare? Not at all! Bark comes in so many different colors, textures, and thicknesses that naturalists can tell what kind of trees they're looking at even in the middle of winter.

In winter, when many trees have lost their leaves, flowers, and fruits, it's easy to see just how many different kinds of bark there are. Bark is like a tree's skin. It's the outermost layer of its trunk and branches. Bark is usually less than a few inches thick, and it protects all the layers of wood inside.

The outer bark you can see protects the tree from damage during snowstorms, fires, and floods. It also insulates during cold winter months and helps retain moisture during hot, dry times. The next layer, the inner bark, lies just below and contains phloem, tube-filled tissue that carries the sugar made by the leaves to the rest of the tree.

What's Underneath?

Just beneath the inner bark is the sapwood, which is made up of xylem, the tissue that carries water and minerals up from the roots, through the trunk and branches, and out to the leaves. Beneath the sapwood, at the center of the trunk, is the heartwood, which is older xylem tissue. It no longer transports water but still helps support the tree.

Bark Up the Right Tree

Bark may be thick or thin, flaky or shaggy, as smooth as paper or deeply wrinkled. Why are there so many variations? Bark is an **adaptation** that helps trees thrive. Each tree **species** needs particular things from its bark to thrive in the conditions where it grows. Thick bark helps trees hold in moisture. Smooth bark is hard for insects to burrow into. Some trees have bark that sheds regularly, which helps get rid of mosses and lichens that grow on the outside of the tree.

Bark can also make bad-tasting chemicals for protection. Many oaks, for example, have deeply furrowed bark, which is perfect for pests to burrow into. To discourage this, they release bitter compounds called tannins, which keep critters from biting into it.

---

1 American sycamore (*Platanus occidentalis*)
2 Eastern white pine (*Pinus strobus*)
3 Northern red oak (*Quercus rubra*)
4 Sugar maple (*Acer saccharum*)
5 Yellow birch (*Betula alleghaniensis*)
6 Birch bark beetle (*Dryocoetes betulae*)

Beautiful Barks

American Sycamore

Sycamores usually grow near water, so they don't need thick bark to hold moisture in. This tree's smooth brown bark flakes off and reveals patches of green and yellow new bark. It looks similar to the bark of the London plane tree, a close relative that is often planted as a street tree in cities.

Platanus occidentalis

Eastern White Pine

The eastern white pine grows in the Northeast and has adapted to survive long, cold winters. It has deeply furrowed bark that insulates the tree, holds in moisture, and protects against frost. Like many other pine species, the white pine also releases sap to repel insects.

Pinus strobus

Yellow Birch

This tree also grows near water and has thin, papery-smooth bark that sheds by peeling. Yellow birch grows and expands really fast. Scientists think its bark peels off because it cannot keep up with the rest of the tree! Never peel it yourself, though. This would harm the tree.

Betula alleghaniensis

American Hornbeam

No other tree in the forest has a trunk and branches that look like the American hornbeam's. It's sometimes called musclewood because of the deep ripples in its bark, which look like veins or muscles in a person's forearm.

Carpinus caroliniana

Eastern Red Cedar

The eastern red cedar grows in or near swamps, and its shaggy reddish bark sheds in thin, vertical strips. These trees are a gorgeous sight in a snowy winter landscape.

Juniperus virginiana

American Beech

This oak relative has smooth, gray bark. Many American beeches have fallen victim to beech bark disease. It is caused by an insect called the beech scale that eats through the bark, which leaves trees susceptible to fungi that can sicken and kill them.

Fagus grandifolia

Botanical Illustrator

Botanical illustrators are highly skilled artists who notice the small details that make each plant unique.

They must love drawing and plants.

How do naturalists let other people know how plants look? Before there were cameras, they relied on finely detailed illustrations. They still do!

Though photography is an important way to record images of plants, a drawing can sometimes show plant characteristics that a photo can't. For instance, what does a flower look like deep inside? How thick are a plant's underground **rhizomes**, and what do they look like growing in the soil? What do fern **spores**, which are almost too tiny to see with the naked eye, really look like? A botanical illustrator is an artist whose specialty is to create drawings like these. ("Botanical" means having to do with plants.)

It takes a special kind of artist to draw these details clearly and accurately. Most botanical illustrators go to art school and may get college degrees in science. They need a thorough knowledge of the way plants are structured. They make drawings for textbooks, scientific journals, museum displays, and nature guides—like this one!

Botanical illustrators usually begin a drawing by making a pencil sketch, either by looking at the plant itself or a photo. Then they trace it in ink. If the illustration is to be in color, they may paint in watercolors or ink or load it onto a computer and add the color using graphics software.

Many botanical illustrations may also be considered fine art. That's not surprising. After all, what could be more lovely to look at than a realistic drawing of nature?

Snow Days

Winter is a tough time for the birds and mammals that live in the city year-round. They must stay warm and find food in a place that was built for people. How do they manage to do it?

Squirrels and raccoons grow thick coats of fur to keep warm. Robins, sparrows, and other birds grow extra feathers. But keeping warm isn't the biggest concern for winter residents, animals that stay put through the winter instead of migrating to warmer climates. Their big challenge is finding food!

Why is this so difficult? Most edible plants either die in the winter or go **dormant**. Their aboveground parts die back, and their belowground parts "sleep" until spring. Leaves, nectar, fruits, and seeds that birds like robins, jays, sparrows, grackles, and cardinals eat are scarce. Insects, another important food source for birds, have also died or gone dormant.

Finding Food

Some winter residents follow a seasonal diet. They feast on juicy earthworms and insects when the weather is warm and make do with winter berries and stored seeds when it's cold.

What do city mammals do? In their **native habitats**, rats, mice, squirrels, and raccoons store extra body fat for winter and continue to hunt as well as eat the food they've gathered and stockpiled in the fall.

In the city, there isn't much natural green space where these animals can **forage** or look for food. Some of them have become opportunistic eaters—they'll eat almost anything! You've probably seen rats or raccoons looking for meals in garbage bins.

Warming Up

There aren't many natural shelters like hollow trees or rock crevices in the city, so some animals seek winter homes in abandoned buildings, basements, or garages. You might even see a mouse in your kitchen or a ladybug overwintering in your windowsill when temperatures start to drop. By adjusting to their environment, these animals are able to make the city their home year-round!

---

1 Pagoda tree (*Styphnolobium japonicum*)
2 Witch-hazel cultivar (*Hamamelis × intermedia* 'Jelena')
3 Downy woodpecker (*Picoides pubescens*)
4 Eastern cottontail (*Sylvilagus floridanus*)
5 Northern cardinal (*Cardinalis cardinalis*)
6 Raccoon family (*Procyon lotor*)
7 Abandoned nest of bald-faced hornet (*Dolichovespula maculata*)
8 Squirrel drey

Help Research Birds

You can help scientists conduct their research by setting up a birdfeeder and keeping track of the bird species that come by to visit.

You can help ornithologists, scientists who specialize in birds, conduct their research by becoming a citizen scientist. Researchers often enlist the help of ordinary citizens to gather all kinds of data on plant or animal populations. One of these projects is called FeederWatch. The ornithologists who started it are interested in tracking the populations of winter resident birds in North America.

They have enlisted citizen scientists from all over North America to set up birdfeeders in winter and keep track of the birds that come and go. Many people in many locations are collecting this information, so the ornithologists have a good sense of how robust the populations of certain species are.

If they notice that a **species** is in trouble, they can start looking into possible causes and sound the alarm that special protection is needed. Visit FeederWatch.org to find out how you can participate.

City Slickers

Downy Woodpecker

This six-inch-tall woodpecker hangs out with birds of
other species in the winter. Why? Sticking together
makes it easier for all of them to stay safe from predators
and find food. Downy woodpeckers peck quietly when
foraging for insects and seeds. You probably won't hear
any loud pecking in winter. Come spring, their loud
knocking is a form of communication that helps the
male establish its territory and attract a mate.

*Picoides
pubescens*

Eastern Gray Squirrel

After spending a busy fall fattening up on acorns and
seeds, the grey squirrel is ready for the winter. When it's
cold, it curls up with other squirrels in tree cavities—
often abandoned woodpecker nests—or in dreys, nests
they build themselves with sticks and leaves high up
in the branches of trees. A squirrel's keen memory and
super sense of smell help it find the stores of nuts and
seeds it buried or hid earlier in the year.

Sciurus carolinensis

Northern Cardinal

Many brightly colored birds molt and grow drab
feathers for better camouflage in winter. Not the
cardinal! The male keeps its flashy feathers. Its bright
color helps attract a mate in early spring. Females are
always brown. Since food is scarce in winter, cardinals
rely on whatever berries are left, like snowberry and
sumac. These berries are bitter, but they become less so
after they freeze and thaw a few times.

Female

Male

Cardinalis cardinalis

What's Up, Bud?

Trees may look lifeless in the winter, but amazing things are happening inside them. Even though spring seems a long way off, leaves and flowers have already formed and are slowly getting ready to burst open.

Scratch a healthy twig with your fingernail. The layer just beneath the surface is usually bright green or yellow and smells fragrant, like a summer garden. It is still very much alive and waiting to transport nutrients and water up to the buds in spring. Healthy trees are covered in buds that formed during the previous summer. You can find them along and at the ends of the tree's twigs.

Tucked Away, Waiting

Buds can be big and knobby, pointy or round, bright purple, yellow, pink, or green. Some are so small they are almost invisible. Inside each one, the leaves or flowers that will emerge in spring have already formed. In winter, they are miniature, scrunched-up versions of what they will eventually become.

Most buds have a tough covering of scales that protects these tiny leaves and flowers by insulating against the cold and keeping harsh winds from drying them out. Some scales are fuzzy, like a sweater. Others are hard and shiny, like armor. Many buds contain gooey gums and resins, which keep them from freezing and make them waterproof.

As spring approaches, the tree starts to send more of the water and sugar it has stored in its trunk and roots up through the branches and out to the buds in the form of sap. (This sweet, running sap is what farmers collect from maple trees this time of the year to make syrup.)

Soon the buds will "burst." They grow fatter as the tissues fill with water and sugar, and the bud scales open. Then the leaves or flowers begin to open. The cells of the leaves expand to their full size, almost like balloons being inflated in slow motion.

Did You Know?

Most trees only open up about half of their buds in early spring. The rest are kept closed as backup in case the first round of buds is eaten by animals or frozen during a spring cold snap.

1 Ash (*Fraxinus* species)
2 Hobblebush (*Viburnum lantanoides*)
3 Red twig dogwood (*Cornus sericea*)
4 Scarlet oak (*Quercus coccinea*)
5 Eastern chipmunk (*Tamias striatus*)

Force a Branch to Come to Life

You can trick branches into thinking it's spring by warming them up and exposing them to light and water. Then watch them leaf out or bloom.

Winter buds need the longer, warmer days of spring to open. They need lots of water, which becomes available when ice and snow melt.

To get a preview, in January and February, harvest some small branches from a few different trees outside. Ask an adult which trees you can use for your experiment. You will also need an adult's help to use pruners or kitchen scissors to cut off a small branch so that you don't damage the tree. Many florists and supermarkets also sell branches of pussy willow, forsythia, quince, and other flowering trees and shrubs in early spring. These will work nicely too.

Bring the branches indoors, and place them in a vase of water in a warm, sunny spot. Watch them over a few weeks, refreshing the water in the vase every few days, and see what happens! Some branches are "forced" more easily than others. Spring-blooming trees like cherry and peach put on the best show.

Some of the Best Buds

Ash

The big, fat bud on the end of a twig is called a "terminal" bud. On ash trees, the chocolate-brown terminal buds look like Hershey's kisses. Terminal buds contain leaves or flowers and also a tiny section of twig, which is ready to shoot out and make the branch longer. Sometimes there are even more buds tucked inside the terminal bud.

Fraxinus species

Hobblebush

Hobblebush buds are "naked"—they have no scales covering them. Instead, they have their own antifreeze chemical inside. Hobblebush, or witch-hobble, gets its name because it is easy to trip over the gangly stems. It is a low shrub, so the buds are at eye level. Look for the crinkly baby leaves sticking out in the cold winter air. Moose and deer eat them to get through winter.

Viburnum lantanoides

Butternut

Each small, fuzzy bud on this tree is located just above a shallow marking called a "leaf scar." This is where last season's leaf was attached to the twig before it fell off. Each leaf scar pattern is different, so you can use it to help identify tree **species** in winter. On a butternut tree, the leaf scar looks like a tiny monkey's face.

Juglans cinerea

Glossary

Adaptation A trait that enhances survival and reproduction or that makes an organism better equipped for a particular environment. An underground **rhizome** is an adaptation that allows plants to survive in areas prone to wildfire.

Awn A long, bristle-like appendage on a plant, such as those on the flowers and **seeds** of many grasses. Awns help the plant spread seeds, for example, by attaching to the fur of animals.

Bract A special leaf at the base of a flower that helps protect it. Bracts are usually smaller than the plant's other leaves and some are very showy. Poinsettias, for example, have bright red bracts, which many people mistake for petals.

Compound leaf A divided leaf consisting of two or more leaflets growing on the same stalk.

Deciduous plant A plant that loses all its leaves for part of the year. In temperate regions such as the northeastern U.S., deciduous trees and shrubs usually drop their leaves in response to cold weather. In tropical climates, leaf drop usually happens during the dry season.

Decompose To break down, rot, or decay. Decomposer organisms, such as many fungi and bacteria, break down dead organic matter like plant parts and animal bodies into simpler forms of matter, making nutrients available for living organisms.

Dioecious plant A species that has male and female reproductive parts, such as flowers or cones, on separate plants. Hollies, willows, and ginkgos are dioecious. (Also see **monoecious**.)

Domesticate To breed and raise an animal or plant for human use. Most of the fruits, vegetables, and grains we eat are domesticated versions of plants originally found in the wild.

Dormancy A period in the life cycle of an organism when growth or activity temporarily slows or stops. **Deciduous** trees go dormant in winter due to freezing temperatures and shorter day length. Many mammals go dormant, or hibernate, in winter to cope with food shortages.

Ecology A branch of science focusing on the relationships among living things and their interactions with their surroundings.

Ecosystem A community of living things plus the nonliving things with which they interact. A pond ecosystem includes the water in the pond, the muck at the bottom, the plants that grow in the water and along the shore, the animals that live there, and those that visit to **forage** for food.

Endangered species A **species** whose populations have declined to the point that it is at high risk of becoming extinct (disappearing forever). Hunting or harming it is forbidden by laws, and usually its **habitat** and food sources are protected.

Evolve To undergo a change in characteristics, or traits, over many generations. New traits first appear spontaneously due to genetic changes. If a new trait (such as a larger beak or a deep **taproot**) helps a plant or animal survive and reproduce in its environment, then it has an advantage over others of its kind. These advantages make that organism more likely to produce offspring and pass down the trait to the next generation.

Feral A **domesticated** animal that has gone back to living in the wild for a generation or more. Unlike stray animals or pets that have been lost or abandoned, feral animals are born in the wild. A feral cat, for example, may be the offspring or descendant of a stray cat.

Forage To search for food. The term is also used to describe plant material eaten by grazing livestock, such as cattle.

Genus, plural **genera** A group of closely related **species**. For example, all the different oak species—there are about 600 of them—belong in the oak genus. The genus name is the first in the two-part scientific name of a species and always starts with a capital letter. For oaks, the genus name is *Quercus*. (Also see **species**.)

Gymnosperm A plant that bears "naked seeds," or **seeds** that are exposed—unlike a flowering plant, which bears seeds enclosed in a fruit. The seeds of gymnosperms develop on the scales of cones or at the end of short stalks. Conifers, cycads, and ginkgos are all gymnosperms.

Habitat The natural environment in which a plant or animal normally lives. This encompasses physical features like soil type, temperature, and moisture levels as well as the dominant plants. Deserts, lakes, forests, and meadows are all different types of habitat.

Herbivore An animal that feeds only on plants. Herbivores, such as deer, often have large, flat, wide teeth, which help them chew grass, bark, and other tough plant material.

Invasive species A nonnative **species** brought to a new **habitat** by people—either intentionally or accidentally—that disrupts that habitat by outcompeting or attacking the **native** plants or animals. Many invasive species have traits such as fast growth and rapid reproduction that enable them to quickly take over new habitats. In their new homes, invasives may have few or no natural enemies to keep them in check.

Larva, plural **larvae** The immature form of any animal that undergoes **metamorphosis** into an adult. Tadpoles are the larvae of frogs, and caterpillars are the larvae of butterflies.

Lichen An organism made up of a **symbiotic** partnership between a fungus and an alga. The alga provides sugar through **photosynthesis**, and the fungus helps absorb water and nutrients. Lichens grow on trees, rocks, soil, and sand in many places, including deserts and polar plains.

Metamorphosis The process by which certain animals undergo significant changes in their body structure and often their behavior as they become adults. Many insects, amphibians, and crustaceans undergo metamorphosis; for example, tadpoles metamorphose into frogs.

Migratory species An animal that moves from one place to another, usually in response to changes in the weather and the availability of **habitat** and food. Every year, many bird **species** migrate north or south with the seasons.

Mycelium, plural **mycelia** The vegetative structure of a fungus, made up of a network of fine, branching filaments called hyphae. Much of the mycelium is found underground.

Mycorrhiza, plural **mycorrhizae** A **symbiotic** relationship between many plants and some **species** of fungi. The fungus grows into the plant's roots and helps the plant take in water and nutrients. Meanwhile, the plant provides food (sugar) to the fungus.

Naturalist Someone who studies plants and animals by observing them directly in nature and tries to understand how these organisms relate to each other and their environment.

Native A plant or animal that occurs in an area naturally—without being brought in by people.

Nymph The immature form of certain insects that undergo a gradual kind of **metamorphosis** before reaching adulthood. Unlike a typical **larva**, a nymph looks a lot like an adult form, but it may be smaller and lack wings or certain internal characteristics.

Photosynthesis The process by which plants capture the energy of sunlight and store it in the form of sugar, used to fuel activities such as growth and reproduction. The green pigment chlorophyll, abundant in most plant leaves, carries out photosynthesis by absorbing light energy and using it to transform carbon dioxide and water into sugar and oxygen.

Pollination The act of moving pollen from a male flower part to a female flower part. After pollination, fertilization can occur, allowing the plant to produce **seeds**. Insects, birds, and bats pollinate plants. So do wind and water.

Pollinator An animal, such as a bee or bird, that moves pollen from the male part of one flower to the female part of another flower.

Rhizome A horizontal plant stem that produces both roots and leafy shoots. Iris, bamboo, ginger, asparagus, and many grasses form rhizomes. They may grow sideways beneath the surface of the soil, enabling plants to spread.

Seed A dormant, baby plant enclosed in a protective outer coating. Seeds often contain a food source that the baby plant uses to emerge from its seed coat and begin to grow, in a process called germination. Making seeds is one important way that plants reproduce and spread. (Also see **vegetative reproduction**.)

Sorus, plural **sori** A cluster of sporangia (saclike structures that produce and contain **spores**) on the underside of fertile fern fronds.

Spathe A large **bract**, or modified leaf, enclosing the flower spike of a member of the arum family of plants, which includes skunk cabbage and Jack-in-the-pulpit.

Species A group of animals, plants, or other organisms related closely enough to interbreed, or produce babies. Members of the same species have traits in common that distinguish them from similar species. (Also see **genus**.)

Spore A reproductive cell or body found in ferns, algae, mosses, and fungi. Spores are capable of developing into new organisms without having to fuse with other reproductive cells.

Stomata Tiny pores in the outer layer of a plant's leaves and stems that allow for the exchange of gases such as carbon dioxide (necessary for **photosynthesis**) and oxygen between the plant and its external environment.

Succession The gradual change in a **habitat** over time. Disturbances like fire and flooding can suddenly remove most of the plants from a site, but a complex community will gradually rebuild itself. Usually, fast-growing but short-lived plants, like grasses, will move in first. Eventually slower-growing but longer-lived plants, like trees, take over.

Succulent A plant with thick, fleshy leaves, stems, or roots adapted to store water. Most, such as cactuses and aloes, live in deserts or on beaches, where fresh water is scarce.

Symbiosis A close relationship between two or more **species**. Symbiosis can be beneficial to all organisms in the relationship or to just one of them. A **lichen** is a symbiotic organism composed of a fungus and an alga in which both partners benefit.

Taproot A stout, tapering, primary root that anchors a plant in soil. A carrot is the taproot of the carrot plant.

Threatened species A **species** that is at risk of becoming endangered in the future. (Also see **endangered**.)

Vegetative reproduction The development of a new plant from the roots, stems, or leaves of a parent plant instead of from a **seed** or **spore**. Strawberry plants, for example, can reproduce by sending out aboveground horizontal stems that root into the soil and form new plants.

Tips for Adult Caregivers

This book is written to inspire and equip children to explore nature. Start sharpening your naturalist skills, along with those of the children in your life, in your own neighborhood. Parks, botanic gardens, community gardens, even tree beds and window boxes can provide opportunities to closely observe plants and animals. Most adventures in this book can be experienced right at home or within a couple of hours of most cities in the Northeast.

Improve Your Chances of Success

Look in the right place at the right time. The adventures in this book are listed by season and habitat. Pay attention to these cues to avoid disappointment. Choose a focus for your walk, such as pollinators, fungi, or tracks. It's hard to see everything at once.

Open your eyes and close your mouth. Loud voices and footsteps will drive away most wildlife, and conversation can distract you from your surroundings. Designate a few minutes of your excursions for watching and listening without talking. Walking your dog and being a naturalist work best as separate outings.

Be a Responsible Explorer

Do no harm and leave no trace. Only collect objects when doing so will not damage a living organism or the environment. Do not give in to the impulse to "rescue" small animals by taking them home. Spring wildflowers wilt within minutes, so don't pick them. Bird feathers and eggs are protected by law, as are endangered or threatened species.

Know the rules of the land. Who owns or manages the land you're exploring? What do they require of visitors? Teach your children to be respectful of rules regarding hours, fees, trails, collecting, pets, and food.

Know When to Steer Clear

Avoid troublesome plants. Many wild plants and fungi are poisonous, so don't explore nature with your taste buds! Most thorns and prickles are easily visible, so you'll know not to touch. Staying on a well-groomed trail will help keep you out of harm's way. Learn to identify these three innocuous-looking but toxic plants:

Poison ivy grows as a vine along the ground or up trees, with clusters of three leaflets 2 to 12 inches long. Don't touch any part of this plant.

Poison sumac is an uncommon shrub or small tree found in wetlands. It causes more severe symptoms than its relative poison ivy.

Stinging nettle is a two- to four-foot-tall weed commonly found in moist areas. Its leaves and stems look downy soft, but some of the hairs carry a strong irritant.

Poison ivy (*Toxicodendron radicans*)

Poison sumac (*Toxicodendron vernix*)

Stinging nettle (*Urtica dioica*)

Watch out for pests. Most animals are busy avoiding you, but if you do encounter a large mammal, keep a safe distance so it doesn't feel threatened. The most common dangers come from some of the smallest species.

Yellow jackets are wasps that build underground nests. They are much more aggressive than most other stinging wasps and bees and may send out a swarm to defend the colony. If you realize you're being chased by more than one wasp, run away as fast as you can.

Blacklegged ticks can transmit several diseases to humans through their bite. They can be smaller than a sesame seed and may remain attached to your skin undetected for several days. Make a point of checking yourself and your children thoroughly after a nature exploration. To lower your risk of contact, stay on the path, tuck long pant legs into your socks, and use insect repellent on your clothing. See a doctor if you or your child develop a rash, fever, or muscle aches.

Be Ready for Adventure

Plan for the weather. Some habitats will be cooler or warmer than your neighborhood, at least for part of the day. Dress in layers so you can make adjustments. Wear sturdy, comfortable shoes. Know when the sun sets, and check the weather forecast before you go.

Prepare to be comfortable. Pick up a trail map if one's available. A knapsack supplied with rain ponchos, sunscreen, water bottles, and wide-brimmed hats can make all the difference between a joyful outing and misery. Carry insect repellent, but only use it if necessary.

Pack your nature exploration kit. See page 9 for some of the things you might want to bring.

Exploring nature costs little to nothing, requires no special equipment, and can be enjoyed by the entire family together. The more time you do it, the more rewarding it becomes.

Contributors

David William Daly was Brooklyn Botanic Garden's Children's Garden coordinator from 2009 to 2014. He's also an avid backpacker and chile pepper enthusiast.

Niall Dunne is a former staff editor at BBG and the editor of four books for the Garden, most recently, *Easy Compost*. He currently directs publishing for the Washington Park Arboretum in Seattle.

Sara Epstein coordinates Project Green Reach, BBG's outreach program in Title I elementary and middle schools throughout Brooklyn. She enjoys hiking with her family in the nature-filled streets, gardens, and parks of NYC, as well as beyond the city limits.

Ashley Gamell manages BBG's Discovery Garden. In her work at the Garden since 2006, she has also curated its Children's Garden and Education greenhouses. A naturalist, horticulturist, and educator, she loves inspiring learners of all ages to discover the science of the natural world.

Patricia Hulse manages the Children's Garden and Family Programs at BBG. She has been exploring the wonders of science and nature with children and adults in urban, suburban, and rural environments since 1995.

Barbara Kurland, manager of School Programs and Partnerships at BBG, has learned much about plants and the natural world by exploring them with children, youth, and adults.

Becky Beer Laboy is an environmental educator and former teacher education coordinator for BBG. She has a passion for wildlife and a commitment to connecting kids with nature.

Saara Nafici coordinates the Garden Apprentice Program at BBG. She is a longtime activist, feminist, bicyclist, naturalist, and youth educator.

Sarah Schmidt edits BBG's Guides for a Greener Planet series and writes interpretive material for the Garden. She loves hiking, camping, and exploring the outdoors with her two curious, nature-loving daughters.

Marilyn Smith, director of Children's Education at BBG, has worked in the field of environmental education for over 25 years. She's an avid naturalist who explores new habitats every chance she gets.

Laszlo Veres has been illustrating books for children since 1987. His favorite themes are historical sailing ships and the natural world.

Additional Illustrations

Manny Jose pages 15, 35, 57, 60, 68, 72, 87, 105